Davide Montingelli
Translated by Kirsten Gallagher

THE RESURGENCE OF ROME

WHAT THE US CAN LEARN FROM THE STRATEGY OF AN EMPIRE ON THE BRINK OF DISASTER

*The successful formula that allowed
the world's first superpower to rise again
from its darkest time in history*

1

To History

3

Introduction

On breaks during my university studies, I often passed by the Roman ruins in Milan. It was pleasant contemplating them. I stayed quite a while imagining how imposing the Maximian's Palace once was.

I have always wondered if the many people who walk by there every day know that the fate of our world was decided over those few stones. It may seem strange but Milan, known for being, among a thousand other things, one of the world's fashion capitals, played a crucial role in ancient history. In the rooms of that very building, in Mediolanum (the latin name of Milan), located today on Via Brisa, politicians and generals from all corners of the globe worked together to save the empire from an unstoppable force: its decline. The Romans were not the first to face such a challenge. Since the birth of the first supranational entities, the threat of decline has been a major concern of citizens and rulers alike. From the moment an empire reached the peak of its splendour, decline has long stimulated profound anxiety.

"When will the end come?" This is the question that the most powerful political actors in history have asked themselves, from Sumerian officials in the third millennium before Christ to the Pentagon's military advisers today[1]. Given the multitude of unforeseen factors that influence the course of history, it is impossible to calculate in a scientific manner how and when the decline of a great power will take place, just as it is impossible to circumvent the decline itself. Empires and nations are much like living organisms: first, they are born, then they grow and age, then they decline, and finally, they perish. So, what can be done about it?

---

[1] S. Mazzarino, *La fine del mondo antico* (1959), Bollati Boringhieri, 2016, pp. 15-17.

This book will focus precisely on responding to this question and attempt to learn if it is at all possible for an imperial or hegemonic force to decelerate this natural process. To do this, we will analyse a dark period in Roman history: The Crisis of the Third Century. Anarchy and invasions were the order of the day; emperors only lasted a few months before being murdered; and civil society had been hopelessly led astray. How did Imperial Rome manage to recover from such a dire situation? What were the measures undertaken by the political actors in Rome to halt the decline? Did the empire really manage to return to form afterwards?

By delving into historical sources and examining interpretations offered by modern theories of international relations, we will seek answers to these questions, not only to bring this period into relief but, more importantly, to determine if it is possible to gain knowledge useful to today's great powers. It is an opportunity to better understand a momentous event in history, the resurgence of Rome, which, even today, scholars look at with wonder and amazement.

First Chapter

The Decline of Empires

Geographical and moral overexpansion

Before plunging into an analysis of the particularities of the decline of the Roman Empire, it will be useful to look at the general concept of decline and what it has meant over time. Once only within the purview of historians, this concept is now debated by scholars of international politics and geopolitics. Not surprisingly, discussion of decline has looked towards what is currently the global hegemonic power, the United States of America. Overseas, theories about decline have been articulated in a number of important writings, including the influential works "The Rise and Fall of the Great Powers" by Paul Kennedy and "War and Change in International Politics" by Robert Gilpin.

The former reveals a trend common among all imperial powers that emerged from the 1500s to the present day; that is, as soon as an established power loses, or fails to develop, its economic-commercial base, its military capacity is significantly blunted. As a result, conflict is created over resources, while massive costs related to running the empire precipitate its decline and eventual fall[2]. This is precisely what happened in Habsburg Spain, France under Louis XIV, the Austro-Hungarian Empire and the Soviet Union[3].

Imperial overstretch[4], as it is called by Kennedy, is thus a systemic problem from which all imperial domains could potentially suffer.

---

[2] P. Kennedy, *The Rise and Fall of Great Powers*, Unwin Hyman Limited, London, 1988.
[3] Ibidem.
[4] Ibidem, p. 515.

In order to illustrate imperial overstretch, we will examine what occurred in the Habsburg Empire, which happens to be the first case presented by the British historian. Despite the vastness of its European territories and the sizeable income derived from mines in the New World, the Habsburgs suffered serious economic difficulties for decades.

"As a result of his various campaigns (...) Charles V realized that all of the different revenues could in no way cover the expenses and that they would be promised to bankers for years to come. (...) His campaign in Metz in 1552 alone cost 2.5 million ducats, a figure ten times greater than the revenues that the emperor expected from the Americas at that time.[5]"

In spite of the fact that the revenues were clearly inadequate, the Habsburg rulers never dared to scale down their undertakings. Instead, they increased them, bringing the empire under greater strain that would eventually topple it.

"The Habsburgs simply had too much to do, too many enemies to fight, too many fronts to defend. The loyalty of the Spanish troops could not compensate for the fact that forces were dispersed among garrisons at home, in North Africa, in Sicily and Italy, in the New World and obviously, in the Netherlands. (...) The Habsburg Empire was a conglomerate of largely dispersed territories, a political and dynastic tour de force that required prolonged physical effort and ingenuity to move forward. As such, (this situation) constituted one of the clearest examples of strategic overstretch in history. The price of having so many territories was the existence of innumerable threats...[6]"

The courage of the troops can never make up for a lack of supplies. In fact, according to Kennedy, wars are won by those who can better endure attrition. It is similar for empires. Spanish political actors never sought to reduce military spending for fear that a retreat from one of their domains would cause a devastating domino effect for their empire[7].

---

[5] Ibidem, p. 46.
[6] Ibidem, p. 50.
[7] Ibidem, pp. 41-55.

However, the simple fact of the matter is, says Kennedy, that pulling out of a troubled area like the Netherlands (we will analyse this case in detail in the last chapter) would have avoided a continuous state of war that in less than a hundred years immersed Spain in a veritable blood bath[8].

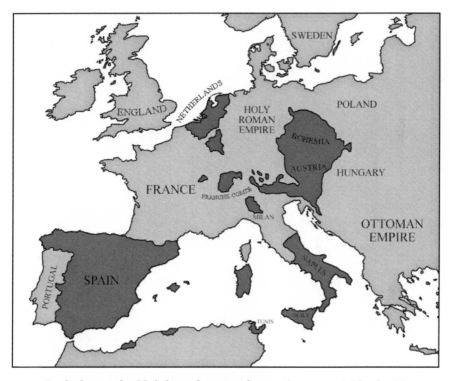

In dark grey the Habsburg domains during the reign of Charles V.
It can be seen that the territories were not contiguous,
which made the empire difficult to defend.
(©Davide Montingelli)

---

[8] Ibidem.

In short, being trapped in a series of costly territorial commitments that are difficult to manage is the greatest possible danger that a great power can face. Robert Gilpin looks at the issue from a different, but no less useful perspective. "War and Change in International Politics" offers intriguing insights on the subject that are grounded in science[9]. For our purposes, the most important observation of Gilpin's theory is undoubtedly the fourth.

"Once this equilibrium position is reached, developments both internal to the dominant power and in its external environment begin to undermine it. In consequence, there is a tendency for the economic costs of maintaining the international status quo to rise faster than the financial capacity of the dominant power to support its position and the status quo.[10]"

Several participants in my cultural association "Renovatio Imperii" have insisted on the opposite; for example, I heard one say, "the empire would not have fallen if it had continued to expand". However, this is incorrect. Domination brings not only benefits, but also costs. If initially, the former exceeds the latter, it encourages expansion; however, over time, the balance starts to shift until a complete reversal is produced. According to Gilpin, there are two categories of factors related to decline, one structural and the other external, that accelerate the inevitable. Regarding the first, the American political scientist offers the historical example of several imperial entities, including that of the Roman Empire. Rome saw its status as a Mediterranean superpower undermined due to the erosion of its economic base (agriculture was never improved through innovation). Its military costs also grew considerably (in the Low Empire mercenaries became increasingly important over time)[11]. These structural factors were compounded by a growing and immoderate demand for consumer goods, a reduction in the economy's productivity and moral decadence that we will discuss in greater detail later on.

---

[9] Robert Gilpin, *War and Change in International Politics*, Cambridge University Press, Cambridge (UK), 1981.

[10] Ibidem, p. 156.

[11] Ibidem, pp. 174-185.

The second category of factors that influenced the decline was external.

"The decreasing profitability of the status quo imposes severe financial burdens on empires and hegemonic powers. The costs of armies, navies and foreign wars are non-productive expenditures; they constitute a balance-of-payments drain on the economy. (...) If this financial problem cannot be resolved, it undermines the economic and military position of the imperial or hegemonic power.[12]"

Further worsening this situation created by the "increasing costs of political dominance [13]" there may also be a loss of economic-technological supremacy, a factor that very often affects empires in decline.

The works of these two great scholars have been immense contributions to the theory of decline. However, it would be a mistake to stop here. Given our goal, it is necessary to go further back in time in order to learn what interpretations of this delicate subject were proffered by the ancients.

The first to provide a careful and analytical account of a declining power was the Greek historian Thucydides. Discussing the violent hegemonic war between Sparta and Athens, known to history as the Peloponnesian War, Thucydides identifies the reasons that brought about the Athenians' end. One famous passage from his work is the Melian Dialogue [14], negotiations between the Athenians and the inhabitants of the island of Melos, who had refused to side with either of the two conflicting parties. This episode was the historian's dramatization of supposed events (it is not known with any certainty if they did indeed occur) serving to compare crucial and contrasting concepts such as morality and political necessity. The gist of the story is the following: The Athenians could not tolerate the Melians' neutrality without weakening their position; the Melians invoked divine law as a means of protection; however, the Athenians, in comparison, subscribed to the much more concrete "law of the strongest".

---

[12] Ibidem, p. 169.
[13] Ibidem, p. 168.
[14] Thucydides, *The Peloponnesian War*, 5, 84-116.

11

The island was eventually decimated, and the survivors sold as slaves. The conquest of Melos, in the Thucydidean narrative, represents the culmination of Athenian power. Shortly, the disastrous expedition against Syracuse will be detailed. In Sicily, Athens lost almost all its war fleet and almost a third of the city's inhabitants[15].

Without the maritime supremacy that had delivered Athens victory over the Persians during the Battle of Michale[16] and with the loss of its status as the pre-eminent power on the Hellenic peninsula, the Athenians slowly crumpled under the assaults of the Peloponnesian League. The massacre perpetrated against the Melians, seen as an absolute necessity from the Athenian point of view (a clear example of *realpolitik* according to numerous political scientists[17]), actually hid what was the beginning of Athens' decline.

In addition to the modern political-philosophical thought of "The Peloponnesian War", Thucydides uses classic *topos* drawn from the Hellenic literary tradition. He employs the concept of *Hybris*, symbolizing pride, excess and transgression (opposed to *Dike*, the goddess of Justice). The actions taken against the Melians by the Athenians were reckless, driven by arrogance underlying Athenian imperial policy. This arrogance would have far-reaching and fatal repercussions for ongoing conflicts elsewhere. First, the Athenians undertook a hasty expedition in Sicily, which represented a turning point in the war, and then later, suffered enormous losses during the Battle of Aegospotami, the final chapter of the struggle between Athens and Sparta. The historian Xenophon[18] reflects on this final battle and what it meant to the Athenians who, in the wake of their defeat,

---

[15] Ibidem, 6-7.

[16] The Battle of Michale (479 B.C.) was a conflict that, along with the Battle of Plataea that same year, effectively put an end to the Persian attempt to conquer the Hellenic peninsula. It was from that moment that Athens began its ascent as a hegemonic-imperial power.

[17] Arthur M. Eckstein, "Thucydides, the Outbreak of the Peloponnesian War, and the Foundation of International Systems Theory", *The International History Review*, Vol. 25, No. 4 (Dec. 2003), pp. 757-774.

[18] Authorship of some parts of the *Hellenica* is still an open question today. In fact, it appears that Xenophon continued the writings of Thucydides.

mourned the end of their domination and questioned their treatment of the Melians.[19]

"(...) during that night no one slept, all mourning, not for the lost alone, but far more for their own selves, thinking that they would suffer such treatment as they had visited upon the Melians, colonists of the Lacedaemonians[20]".

Almost ten years later, the yet unknown consequences weighed heavily on Athenian minds. According to Thucydides, it was a horrific crime. Even if it did not directly cause the downfall of Athens, it was certainly representative of its end from a moral point of view.

There is another Greek whose writings follow in the Thucydidean tradition: Polybius[21]. The historian, transplanted to Rome after the Macedonian Wars, was the noble and "pragmatic[22]" narrator of the rise of Rome in the Mediterranean. In his "Histories," a theory that is called *anakyklosis* in Greek is formulated, which describes a cyclic evolution of political regimes. Initially, Polybius did not think Rome was going to evolve in the same way due to its mixed constitution and the fact that it balanced three "benign" forms of government; however, time and maturity rendered the historian and his analysis much more astute:

"That all existing things are subject to decay and change is a truth that scarcely needs proof; for the course of nature (κατά φύσιν) is sufficient to force this conviction on us. There being two agencies by which every kind of state is liable to decay, the one external and the other a growth of the state itself, we can lay down no fixed rule about the former, but the latter is a regular process. (...) And what will happen is, I think, evident. When a state has weathered many great perils and subsequently attains to supremacy and uncontested sovereignty, it is evident that under the influence of long-

---

[19] The Battle of Aegospotami (405 B.C.) was the battle that marked the end of the Peloponnesian War. The Athenian fleet was completely destroyed by the Spartans.

[20] Xenophon, *Hellenica*, II, 2, 3.

[21] Polybius (206 B.C. - 124 B.C.) was a Greek historian who chronicled the rise of Rome in the Mediterranean. In his "Histories," the clashes between the Romans and the Carthaginians were given particular attention.

[22] Polybius defines his historiography as "pragmatic" because it is based on objective facts (*pragmatà*).

established prosperity, life will become more extravagant and the citizens fiercer in their rivalry regarding office and other objects than they ought to be. As these defects go on increasing, *the beginning of the change for the worse will be due to love of office and the disgrace entailed by obscurity, as well as to extravagance and purse-proud display...*[23]"

Rome, although characterized by relatively greater stability than that of other political entities that followed on the Hellenic peninsula, had to perish, like all things, κατά φύσιν. Its decline would be triggered by that "unquestionable excellence and power" that the *Res Publica* began to flaunt after the Punic Wars. This reading, which does not fully agree with what is written in the first chapters of "Histories[24]", was probably the result of events that Polybius directly witnessed: the first being the social disorder caused by the Gracchi brothers[25] and the second, the destruction of two major cities of the ancient world, Corinth and Carthage[26]. The leaders of the Senate loudly called for these military actions, which the historian from Megalopolis saw as embodying the same imperial arrogance that Thucydides brought to light in the Melian Dialogue. The address of Scipio Aemilianus to Polybius in front of the smoking ruins of Carthage is in this sense very eloquent:

"A glorious moment, Polybius; but I have a dread foreboding that someday the same doom will be pronounced on my own country.[27]"

Scipio's empathy was rare among a ruling class that, according to Polybius, substituted the values that allowed it to successfully dominate the world with a dangerous presumption, blind to the degeneration and inevitable decline that would be visited upon it. Evidence of changing values is provided in "Histories"; in particular, in Polybius'

---

[23] Polybius, *Histories*, 6, 57.

[24] C. O. Brink and F. W. Walbank, "The Construction of the Sixth Book of Polybius", *The Classical Quarterly*, Cambridge University Press, Cambridge (UK), Vol. 4, No. 3/4 (Jul. - Oct., 1954), pp. 97-122.

[25] Tiberius Sempronius Gracchus and Gaius Sempronius Gracchus were two Roman politicians who fought a political battle against the most aristocratic elements of the Senate to improve the conditions of the people.

[26] Both occured in 146 B.C.

[27] Polybius, *Histories*, 38, 21, 1-3.

description of a Roman diplomatic mission in the Hellenistic East[28].
On this occasion, the Roman legate Gaius Popillius Laenas, who had been sent to mediate between the Ptolemies and the Seleucids, discourteously treated Antiochus IV, sovereign of the Seleucids. Antiochus asked for time to reflect on a message sent by the Roman Senate and Laenas drew a circle in the sand around the king and commanded him not to leave it before providing an answer[29]. Episodes like this, which the historian calls "offensive and exceedingly arrogant[30]", confirmed Polybius' conviction that conquest and greatness lead to reckless arrogance that prevents men from even considering that their empire could fall like countless others in the past[31]. The Polybian theory of decline thus roughly follows the one offered by Thucydides in "The Peloponnesian War". Thucydides argues that once they reach their apogee, all empires suffer from an inability to resist what I call "moral overexpansion". Unlike his fellow countryman, however, Polybius attempts to offer through the *exempla*[32] of temperate individuals who empathize with the sufferings of others (though it should be noted that he looks only to soldiers and statesmen for models of empathy), an antidote that, if not completely preventative, will at least slow decline.

Although the lesson of "moral overexpansion" may be a modern one (consider the Bush administration's incursions in Iraq, for example[33]), the theory of decline has developed a great deal since ancient times, as mentioned at the beginning of the chapter. The blind spot of Thucydides and Polybius as well as other major contributors to historiography, is that they do not consider the purely economic side of

---

[28] R. Balot, "Polybius' Advice to the Imperial Republic", *Political Theory*, Sage Publications, Inc. Vol. 38, No. 4 (August 2010), p. 494.

[29] Polybius, *Histories*, 29, 2, 1-4.

[30] Ibidem, 29, 27, 1-8.

[31] M. Jo Davies, "Polybius on the Roman Republic: Foretelling a Fall," *Saber and Scroll*, 2015, Vol. 4: Iss. 2, Article 9.

[32] R. Balot, "Polybius' Advice to the Imperial Republic", *Political Theory*, Sage Publications, Inc. Vol. 38, No. 4 (August 2010), p. 496.

[33] C.K. Armstrong, *Tyranny of the Weak: North Korea and the World, 1950-1992*, (2013), pp. 291-292 and J. Zumbrunnen, *Silence and Democracy: Athenian Politics in Thucydides' History*, 2010.

imperial decline. This aspect is now recognized as being absolutely fundamental thanks to the development of various methods and analytical tools. First to speak of "overexpansion" in the modern sense was Edward Gibbon[34], in the celebrated "The History of the Decline and the Fall of the Roman Empire". Looking closely at the example provided by Rome, the English historian reaches the conclusion that the most dangerous trap that an empire can fall into is that of taking on commitments and responsibilities without limits.

"The decline of Rome was the natural and inevitable effect of immoderate greatness. Prosperity ripened the principle of decay; the causes of destruction multiplied with the extent of conquest; and as soon as time or accident had removed the artificial supports, the stupendous fabric yielded to the pressure of its own weight. The story of its ruin is simple and obvious; and instead of inquiring why the Roman Empire was destroyed, *we should rather be surprised that it had subsisted so long.*[35]"

The massive expansion of the Roman Empire was both the source of its power and the reason for its decline, Gibbon maintains. The ever-increasing demand on resources to defend the empire reduced the possibility for internal growth.

Gibbon's analysis had contemporary relevance as well as historical implications. The starting point of his work was the Golden Age of the Roman Empire; he thought that his homeland of Great Britain, at that time, was also in the midst of a Golden Age. There was a clear "parallel" lesson that British political actors had to learn if they wanted to avoid a violent collapse like the one that the Western Roman Empire suffered in the fifth century. It is no coincidence that, a century after Gibbon's death, *overextension* became a recurring theme among British intellectuals.

---

[34] H. Münkler, *Empires. World Domination from Ancient Rome to the United States*, il Mulino, 2012, p. 171. Edward Gibbon (1737-1794) was a British politician and author of several historical works. His approach was based very much on the skepticism and rationalism of the Enlightenment.

[35] E. Gibbon, *The History of the Decline and Fall of the Roman Empire*, "General Observations on the Fall of the Roman Empire in the West".

Between the late 1800s and the early 1900s, Britain was beginning to find it difficult to maintain its status as the pre-eminent power on the international scene[36]. The aggression of Germany, the disastrous war against the Boers[37] and economic difficulties led many thinkers, including Rudyard Kipling, Francis Haverfield, Sir Baden Powell and Elliot Mills Evans[38], to enlarge and develop the theory of decline elaborated by Gibbon in his discussion of ancient Rome.

"Studying his seven volumes (of Gibbon's work a/n), as I have recently done, and comparing them with the records of English life from the beginning of the Twentieth Century at its close, I have been almost startled out of my senses by the symptoms of decay common to the two epochs. The only difference, apart from the setting, is that the decline of England was far more rapid. The reason is obvious. There were far more competitors in the field.[39]"

The particular political climate generated from the earlier Victorian Age and the First and Second World Wars allowed the message to penetrate: Great Britain did not allow itself to become drunk on *folie de grandeur* typical of all decaying empires. Instead, the empire initiated a relatively painless and undoubtedly prudent withdrawal from its more expensive domains.

---

[36] K. Rasler and W. R. Thompson, "Relative Decline and the Overconsumption-Underinvestment Hypothesis", *International Studies Quarterly*, Wiley, Vol. 35, No. 3 (Sep., 1991), pp. 273-294 and A. Hartley, "O! What a Fall was There: Reflections on the Decline of Britain", *The National Interest*, Center for the National Interest, No. 35 (Spring 1994), pp. 36-46.

[37] J. G. Darwin, "The Fear of Falling: British Politics and Imperial Decline Since 1900", *Transactions of the Royal Historical Society*, Cambridge University Press, Cambridge (UK), Vol. 36 (1986), pp. 30-32.

[38] R. Kipling (1865-1936) was one of the most famous British writers and poets of his era; Francis Haverfield (1860-1919) was an archaeologist and professor of ancient history at the University of Oxford; Sir Baden Powell (1857-1941) was a military general and educator, known to history as the founder of the Scouting movement; Elliot Evans Mills (1881-1956) was a historian famous mainly for his work, similar in subject to that of Gibbon, entitled "The Decline and Fall of British Empire".

[39] E.E. Mills, *The Decline and Fall of British Empire*, Bocardo Press (1905), London, pp. 3-4.

Portrait of the English historian Edward Gibbon,
the precursor of the concept of "imperial overextension".

Possible solutions to prevent decline

In short, is there really a way to avoid what seems, from Thucydides to Kennedy, an inexorable fall? No cure lasts forever. As mentioned previously, decline is a natural stage in any organism, be it biological or political. Nevertheless, several "anti-decline" measures have been put forward throughout history. These supplement the "moral behaviours" promoted in ancient historiography, such as engaging in preventive war, as discussed in Thucydides.

"The real cause I consider to be the one which was formally most kept out of sight. The growth of the power of Athens, and the alarm which this inspired in Lacedaemon, made war inevitable.[40]"

Frightening the Spartans was, on the one hand, the possible decline of their power and on the other, the expansionism of their Athenian rival[41]. The concept of preventive war is simple: military force is employed to prevent the growth of an antagonist. Unfortunately, the costs of the conflict are high and the outcomes for the future are uncertain[42]. Gilpin thinks of preventive war as a "primary tool for resolving the dilemma of acute decline". According to the author of "War and Change in International Politics," the dominant power in crisis should annihilate the rising challenger when it still has the strength to do so[43]. Broadly practiced by the states of the international system during the first part of the contemporary age, this practice is strongly criticized today.

---

[40] Thucydides, The Peloponnesian War, 1, 23, 6.
[41] J.S. Levy, "Declining Power and the Preventive Motivation for War", World Politics, Cambridge University Press, Cambridge (UK), Vol. 40, No. 1 (Oct., 1987), p. 83.
[42] J.S. Levy, "Preventive War and Democratic Politics", International Studies Quarterly, Blackwell Publishing, Oxford, (2008) 52, pp. 1-24.
[43] Robert Gilpin, War and Change in International Politics, Cambridge University Press, Cambridge (UK), 1981, p.93.

"Powers pursuing preventive war are shouldering grave risks: preventive war may require resources that are unavailable or allies that are difficult to recruit, and defeat in preventive war opens floodgates to exploitation on multiple fronts. Even a successful war, if sufficiently costly, can weaken a great power to the point of vulnerability.[44]"

The Spartan king Archidamus II was keenly aware of this. On the eve of the Peloponnesian War, he warned his fellow citizens that a preventive war against Athens would be drawn-out and involve massive, large-scale efforts. Spartan interventionists did not understand that this type of conflict, given all the factors at play, would have had an unlikely outcome. However, the war was agreed upon in a vote one month after the king spoke against it. Sparta dragged Athens into a bloody hegemonic struggle that lasted almost thirty years. The Spartans had the upper hand but success was ephemeral and the conflict led to exhaustion on both sides[45]. The problem with preventive war is that many, including Gilpin, tend to overestimate its benefits and underestimate its intrinsic danger. On the battlefield, there are always a wild number of unforeseen factors. On this point, the great German statesman Otto Von Bismark was very clear.

"Preventive war is like committing suicide for fear of death.[46]"
"(...) We will have to wait, rifle at rest, and see what clouds of smoke and eruptions the volcano of Europe will produce. We should not follow a policy similar to that of Frederick II at the beginning of the Seven Years' War - attacking an enemy who is preparing to attack. It would in fact be like cracking open eggs from which very dangerous roosters might emerge.[47]"

The only situation in which preventive war can bring appreciable results is when forces are unequal.

---

[44] P. MacDonald and J.M. Parent, "Graceful Decline? The surprising success of Great Power Retrenchment", *International Security*, Vol. 35, No. 4 (Spring 2001), p. 16.

[45] J. Lobel, "Preventive War and Lessons of History", *Less Safe Less Free: The Failure of Preemption in the War on Terror*, University of Pittsburgh Law Review, p. 318.

[46] H. Kahn, *Thinking About the Unthinkable in the 1980s*, 1985, p. 136.

[47] L. Gall, *Bismarck: The White Revolutionary:1815-1871*, p. 519.

The Third Punic war[48] (149 - 146 B.C.) exemplified these circumstances when the Romans completely destroyed Carthage out of fear that the ancient rival would return to the glories of the past. Hannibal's homeland did not represent any threat at that time and Rome carried out the war with relative ease. Though, as mentioned earlier, such cases are rare and the application of preventive war in areas other than this would lead to uncertainties difficult for any power to tolerate.

Far less dangerous and aggressive, and therefore, generally preferred in the context of international relations, is the strategy known as *retrenchment*. Retrenchment is a political strategy aimed at reducing and redistributing a great power's burdens by cutting military spending, reducing obligations to allies and withdrawing from territorial commitments that are too costly to maintain[49]. Some have considered abandoning hegemonic-imperial duties dangerous since it would be a source of worry for friendly powers and be seen as an invitation to shrewd rivals; however, it must be made clear that retrenchment is not a retreat.

"The fact that the Soviet Government had agreed to withdraw their missiles and their aircraft from Cuba was not evidence of weakness but of realism... But Berlin was an entirely different question; not only was it of vital importance to the Soviet Government but the Russians had overwhelming conventional superiority in the area.[50]"

These words, uttered by the former British Prime Minister Harold Macmillan in his Cabinet, clearly express the true spirit of retrenchment: it is not a retreat, but a studied reallocation of resources. If a withdrawal ensues, it always follows that a higher-priority area grows stronger than the one just abandoned.

---

[48] The Third Punic War (149 - 146 B.C.) was the final chapter of the wars waged between Rome and Carthage. It saw the total destruction of the latter and the final annexation of North Africa by the Roman Republic.

[49] P. MacDonald and J.M. Parent, "Graceful Decline? The Surprising Success of Great Power Retrenchment", *International Security*, Vol. 35, No. 4 (Spring 2011).

[50] Ibidem, p. 15.

The commitments[51] of a great power have different and specific weights that are, more importantly, not interdependent. During the Cold War, the Soviet Union shifted military resources from a distant and relatively unimportant territory in Cuba in order to reinforce its presence in more important ones in Europe. It did all of this without suffering the so-called domino effect (one falls, they all fall) which is the worry of those pessimistic about retrenchment. The empirical data show us that, unlike preventive war, retrenchment is a relatively common measure among nations suffering from acute decline. Of fifteen declining powers analyzed in the research of MacDonald and Parent, fully 40% succeeded in recovering their original status thanks to this policy[52]. On the contrary, none of the powers that did not implement retrenchment recovered their former pre-eminent positions[53]. This approach can provide a key to understanding the topic that we will analyze. As mentioned earlier, it is not the end of empires that interests us but rather, the more successful attempts made by powers throughout history to delay the inevitable. And in this sense, it is useful to return to the words of Gibbon: "instead of inquiring why the Roman empire was destroyed, we should rather be surprised that it had subsisted so long".

It is looking at the most widely known and acclaimed imperial entity of all time and drawing from its experience during the period known as the "Crisis of the Third Century" that we will gain important insights relevant to us today.

---

[51] English term which in international relations refers to the territorial commitments of great powers.
[52] Ibidem, p. 10.
[53] Ibidem.

Second Chapter

An Empire in Difficulty: The Landscape of the Third Century

Marcus Aurelius and the end of the Golden Age

Roman difficulties paradoxically began to take shape during a rather happy time for the empire. Delighted by the handover from Antoninus Pius to Marcus Aurelius in A.D. 161, the Roman people seemed to be entering a period that would be marked by good governance and peace. Good governance was expressed in the euergetism[54] of the philosopher emperor but peace was completely disregarded. In fact, Vologases IV, King of Parthia, exploited the succession and overthrew the pro-Roman government of Armenia, wiping out a Roman legion from Cappadocia[55]. In little time all the imperial outposts on the Euphrates fell and the Parthian armies spread throughout territories in Syria, neutralizing all resistance. As if that were not enough, the Picts broke through the Antonine Wall in Britain and a burgeoning movement of

---

[54] The term "euergetism" derives from the Greek εὐεργετέω ("to do good") and makes reference to a practice in use among Roman rulers which consisted of giving gifts to the population.

[55] Historia Augusta, *The Life of Marcus Aurelius*, 8, 6; Cassius Dio, *Roman History*, 71, 2, 1.

new peoples from the Baltics put greater stress on the Germanic limes[56]. The Romans had not had to deal with such a situation for several decades but nevertheless, the new emperor reacted promptly: Marcus Aurelius sent his colleague Lucius Verus to command sixteen legions to curb the expansionism of Vologases[57] and in less than a year, the Romans reconquered Armenia and its capital Artaxata, placing Gaius Julius Sohaemus, who was loyal to Rome[58], on the throne again. They then diverted offensive efforts to the south in the direction of Mesopotamia, repeatedly defeating the Parthians. The campaign ended victoriously in 166, with the conquest of the capital Ctesiphon and the destruction of Vologases' royal palace[59]. Such successes allowed Rome to keep its historical enemy in check for the next thirty years and to bolster the empire's eastern border between the western shore of the Khabur River and the Jabal Sinjar mountain range[60]. There was hardly time to celebrate this triumph since the northern borders, left unguarded during the Parthian expedition, were assaulted by barbarians. Six thousand barbarians from Germanic tribes known as the Lombards and Ubii crossed the Danube, pouring into the Roman province of Upper Pannonia. This force targeted the Roman forts of Arrabona and Brigetio before being quickly intercepted and repulsed by infantry and cavalry from *Legio I Adiutrix* and *Ala I Ulpia Contariorum*[61]. Eleven of the Germanic tribes sent emissaries to Marcus Iallius Bassus, governor of Pannonia, to apologize for the regrettable event and ask for a truce[62]. However, what might have seemed like a mere disturbance actually represented the tip of an imposing and dangerous iceberg that had been long hidden. In fact, in a short amount of time, the incursions in and around the Danube increased exponentially, forcing

---

[56] Historia Augusta, Marcus Aurelius, 8,7.

[57] Ibidem, 8, 12.

[58] Ibidem, 9, 1.

[59] Historia Augusta, *Lucius Verus*, 8, 3-4.

[60] D. Oates, "The Roman Frontier in Northern 'Iraq", *The Geographical Journal*, Vol. 122, No. 2 (Jun., 1956), p. 193 and N.C. Debevoise, *Political History of Parthia*, University of Chicago Press, 1938, pp. 250-254.

[61] Cassius Dio, *Roman History*, 72, 12.

[62] Ibidem.

the two emperors to first recruit two legions in Aquileia, the *II Italica* and *III Italica*[63], and then advance towards the Danube in the direction of the legionary fortress Carnuntum. Months of eerie quiet followed, interrupted only by the death of Lucius Verus[64] (in 169) and a few incursions by the Iazyges in Dacia. As Marcus Aurelius fought the Iazyges, the imperial fears materialized: Ballomar, King of the Marcomanni, leading a coalition of various Germanic tribes, crossed the Danube and promptly defeated the Romans near Carnuntum. There, he gained a foothold and besieged the city of Aquileia[65]. A foreign army had not set foot on Italian soil since 101 B.C., the year Gaius Marius claimed victory on the Campi Raudii against the Cimbri and Teutons. Even if the empire had been assailed elsewhere, in Gaul and the Balkans, for example, the Germanic invasion in Northern Italy became the highest priority for the philosopher emperor. It represented an affront to Roman prestige simply too great to be neglected. This is why Marcus Aurelius put his best generals, Tiberius Claudio Pompeianus and Publius Helvius Pertinax, in charge in the region. They quickly freed Aquileia from the siege and drove back the invaders beyond the Danube. The emperor then established a new military district, the *Praetentura Italiae et Alpium*, to better protect that vulnerable region.

The fall of the Marcomanni is considered significant for three reasons: first, as mentioned earlier, this "inaugural" invasion opened a season of continuous attacks on the empire; second, the barbarians from Germania Magna were mobilizing into leagues and confederations, and gaining confidence for it; third the invasions during this period were not aimed at conquering the territory (as they would be later) but rather, looting it. The situation incited Marcus Aurelius to implement a plan that he likely had in mind for some time. It was a plan to form two new provinces, Marcomannia and Sarmatia in order to retrench a border that was becoming increasingly problematic[66].

---

[63] Ibidem, 55, 24.
[64] Historia Augusta, *Lucius Verus*, 9, 7-11.
[65] Cassius Dio, *Roman History*, 72, 2-3.
[66] Historia Augusta, *Marcus Aurelius*, 24, 5.

Through similar actions, the great threat represented by the Marcomanni and Quadi could be managed and, in addition, the dangerous salient between the Danube and Tisza rivers (left over from the Roman conquest of Dacia fifty years before), vulnerable to three-sided attacks from Sarmatian tribes, could be eliminated. A long and difficult conflict followed, punctuated only by the rebellion of Avidius Cassius in Syria, which saw the Romans advancing in what are now the territories of Moravia, Slovakia and Hungary. Eventually, the Quadi and Marcomanni were defeated, but just as the Romans were preparing to draw borders around new provinces, the philosopher emperor died.

"(Marcus Aurelius) did not meet with the good fortune that he deserved, for he was not strong in body and was involved in a multitude of troubles throughout practically his entire reign. But for my part, I admire him all the more for this very reason, that amid unusual and extraordinary difficulties he both survived himself and preserved the empire. Just one thing prevented him from being completely happy, namely, that after rearing and educating his son in the best possible way, he was vastly disappointed in him. This matter must be our next topic; for our history now *descends from a kingdom of gold to one of iron and rust*, as affairs did for the Romans of that day.[67]"

The ambitious project to create a new *ultra flumen* border thus disappeared together with Marcus Aurelius. Although Cassius Dio's thesis is shared by many historians (Gibbon himself identifies the beginning of the reign of Commodus as the start of the decline of Rome[68]), it would be useful to pause and try to better understand one of the immense trials that Rome faced during this period and the decades that followed it: the *Antonine Plague*. This plague (ancient evidence indicates that it may have been smallpox) was probably brought to the empire by the soldiers of Lucius Verus during the siege of Seleucia, in A.D. 166[69]; it spread to the most northerly provinces, causing death and despair for more than twenty years.

---

[67] Cassius Dio, *Roman History*, 72, 36, 3-4.

[68] E. Gibbon, *The History of the Decline and Fall of Roman Empire*, Ch. 1.

[69] R. J. Littman and M. L. Littman, "Galen and the Antonine Plague", *The American Journal of Philology*, The Johns Hopkins University Press, Vol. 94, No. 3 (Autumn, 1973), pp. 243-255.

Cassius Dio, contemporary historian at the time of the plague, explains that, under Commodus, the plague killed two thousand people in a single day[70], while later authors exaggerated the total fatalities from this *pestilentia*[71]. Speculation about the effects of the disease is ongoing today. There are those who say that it had a devastating impact on the Roman Empire, killing half of its population and contributing decisively to its decline, and there are others who proffer a more moderate estimate, claiming that the effects of the plague were almost marginal, with deaths ranging between 500,000 and 1,000,000 (1-2% of the total population)[72]. What likely happened is somewhere in the middle of these two versions. Mortality surged in crowded milieus like cities and military camps, doing considerable damage, while in others it was better contained. Part of the population was devoted to agriculture, for example, and was kept away from the disease. We can therefore say that the impact of the Antonine Plague was not decisive for the decline of the Roman empire, as many say; however, it did lead to the death of somewhere between 7 and 15 million individuals, which was indeed a severe blow to a society based largely on human strength[73].

---

[70] Cassius Dio, *Roman History*, 72, 14, 3-4.

[71] "...over half of the population of the empire perished; the settlement of the Germans that followed led to fundamental changes of lasting importance": O. Seeck, *Geschichte des Untergangs der antiken Welt*, I, 1910, Stoccarda, pp. 398-405 in S. Sabbatani, S. Fiorino, "The Antonine Plague and the Decline of the Roman Empire. Role of the Parthian War and the Marcomannic Wars between 164 and 182 A.D. in the Spread of the Contagion", *Le Infezioni in Medicina*, 2009, Bologne, No. 4, p. 270, and "...this plague must have hit with incredible fury; it must have claimed countless victims. Since the reign of Marcus Aurelius represented a turning point in so many ways; above all, in art and literature, I have no doubt that this crisis was caused by the plague. The ancient world never recovered from the blow dealt by the plague that visited it during the reign of M. Aurelio ": B.C. Niebuhr, *Lectures on the History of Rome*, Vol. III, p. 251, Lecture CXXI, 1849, London, in Ibidem.

[72] J.F. Gilliam, "The Plague under Marcus Aurelius", *Am. J. Philology*. 327, 1961, pp. 225-251.

[73] R. J. Littman and M. L. Littman, "Galen and the Antonine Plague", *The American Journal of Philology*, The Johns Hopkins University Press, Vol. 94, No. 3 (Autumn,

Evidence that has reached us from Roman Egypt at that time testifies to the fact that the economy was certainly faltering. The price of mules increased by 50% (probably because they were being used for work that sick or dead laborers would have done), the demand for wine and oil decreased, and there was a significant reduction in tax payers in the villages of the Nile Delta[74]. In Italy, as previously mentioned, Marcus Aurelius and Lucius Verus had to recruit two new legions (the *II Italica* and *III Italica*) to remedy the shortage of men caused by the plague.

The Severan Age: the militarization of the state and the metamorphosis of enemies

Fortunately, Commodus did not have to face any serious external threats, partly because the military chain of command was highly efficient and partly because he had successfully signed peace treaties with the Danuban tribes. After twelve years as emperor, the son of Marcus Aurelius was killed by a conspiracy and Pertinax was installed in his place. Pertinax was a skilful military commander but his government, however, lasted only a few months and Rome fell into a five-year civil war. The internal struggles ended in 197 with the Battle of Lugdunum, which culminated in Septimius Severus being named the sole ruler of Rome[75]. Of provincial origin (his father was a native of Leptis Magna, in Tripolitania), the new emperor immediately embraced a despotism characterized by aversion to senatorial order and complete authority over the army.

1973), pp. 243-255.

[74] S. Sabbatani, S. Fiorino, "The Antonine Plague and the Decline of the Roman Empire. Role of the Parthian War and the Marcomannic War between 164 and 182 A.D. in Spreading the Infection", *Le Infezioni in Medicina*, 2009, Bologne, No. 4, pp. 261-275.

[75] Cassius Dio, *Roman History*, 76, 7.

"Distributing large sums of money to the soldiers, he granted them many privileges which they had not previously enjoyed. He was the first emperor to increase their food rations, to allow them to wear gold finger rings, and to permit them to live with their wives; these were indulgences hitherto considered harmful to military discipline and the proper conduct of war. Severus was also the first emperor to make a change in the harsh and healthy diet of the soldiers and to undermine their resolution in the face of severe hardships; moreover, he weakened their strict discipline and respect for their superiors by teaching them to covet money and by introducing them to luxurious living.[76]"

Given the bloody circumstances in which he ascended to power, the emperor wished to ingratiate himself to the army, which he considered to be the only legitimate source of power. To do so, he resorted to continuous increases in pay and concessions. Leaving aside for a moment the criticisms that ancient historians have made of Septimius, his actions could also be seen as a way to encourage higher recruitment rates for the legions. *Pax Romana* and diffuse citizenship had made a military career less and less "attractive" by the end of the second century. That, combined with a shortage of men in the Roman army, could have certainly been justification enough for the actions of Severus[77].

Whatever the real aims of the emperor were, the annual legionary pay increased dramatically. A legionary at the beginning of Augustus' reign received a sum equal to 150 *denarii* but a Roman soldier under Septimius Severus could earn up to 600[78]. Then there were *donativa*, prizes to supplement the *stipendium* (regular pay) that were given to the army on special occasions. Ancient sources tell us that Septimius Severus bestowed three of them[79].

[76] Herodian, *History of the Roman Empire since the Death of Marcus Aurelius*, 3, 8, 4-5.

[77] R. E. Smith, "The Army Reforms of Septimius Severus", *Historia: Zeitschrift für Alte Geschichte*, Franz Steiner Verlag, Bd. 21, H. 3 (3rd Qtr., 1972), pp. 481-500.

[78] P.I. Prodromídis, *Another View on an Old Inflation: Environment and Policies in the Roman Empire up to Diocletian's Price Edict*, Centre of Planning and Economic Research, Athens, February 2006, p. 13.

[79] Herodian, *History of the Roman Empire since the Death of Marcus Aurelius*, 2, 14, 5; Historia Augusta, *Septimius Severus*, 16, 5; Cassius Dio, *Roman History*, 77, 1, 1.

*Septimius Severus, a great innovator of
the military and strategic structure of the empire.*

Finally, as mentioned by Herodian, the emperor granted additional food rations to the soldiers. During the first two centuries of the empire the living costs of a legionary (or auxiliary) were deducted from his *stipendium*; however, under Septimius Severus the food supplies were the financial responsibility of municipal councils [80]. All of these measures employed to win the favour of the army and the costs of the numerous public works commissioned by the emperor were possible because of major changes in the currency. These changes produced more copious amounts of currency (in the first three years of his reign, Septimius circulated 114 different types of *denarii* per year; by comparison, Antoninus Pius had an average of 17 different types per year[81]) and a debasement of the coin. The silver contained in the *denarius* was reduced from 72 to 73% at the beginning of Commodus' reign to 50 to 60% during the last years of his reign[82].

The emperor's expenses did not end there. Another burden on the state budget was the new expedition against Parthia, which had supported a contender to the Roman imperial throne against Septimius during the civil war from 193 to 197. Three new legions[83] (the *I Parthica*, *II Parthica* and *III Parthica*) were recruited for a new expedition to the East. The Romans first committed to pacifying the client kingdoms of Osroene and Adiabene (territories in Iraq and Syria today), who had taken advantage of the empire's volatile political situation to rebel. The city of Nisibis, a Roman stronghold from the time of Lucius Verus, was reconquered, provoking Septimius Severus to divide his army into three to better cover the front of the attack. The campaign was a success but a new contender brought the emperor back to the West.

---

[80] R. I. Frank, "Ammianus on Roman Taxation", *The American Journal of Philology*, The Johns Hopkins University Press Vol. 93, No. 1, Studies in Honor of Henry T. Rowell (Jan., 1972), pp. 71-72.

[81] A. Wassink, "Inflation and Financial Policy under the Roman Empire to the Price Edict of 301 A.D.", *Historia: Zeitschrift für Alte Geschichte*, Franz Steiner Verlag, Bd. 40, H. 4 (1991), p. 478.

[82] K. Butcher, *Debasement and the Decline of Rome*, pp. 182-201.

[83] Cassius Dio, *Roman History*, 55, 24.

The war with the Parthians raged in the summer of 197. Septimius Severus crossed the Euphrates with newly recruited legions, conquering Seleucia, Babylon and finally Ctesiphon, which was burned and sacked by his men[84]. The military operations in the East allowed Rome to further solidify its position. Northern Mesopotamia became a province and the cities of Nisibis and Singara were integrated into the Roman defense system; the new territories provided bridgeheads to cross the Tigris River in potential future invasions[85]. However, Septimius Severus had not realized his loftier ambitions, since the capital Ctesiphon was abandoned almost immediately by the legions and Hatra's valuable outpost was besieged albeit unsuccessfully; there were terrible losses of men, means and provisions[86]. Despite everything, the empire still enjoyed a few years of quietude until the beginning of the third century when another crisis exploded, this time in the West.

Scotland and its tribes had created problems since the building of the Antonine Wall but in recent years the pressure that they were putting on Roman defenses was becoming intolerable. As such, Septimius Severus saw an opportunity for a new military expedition across the Channel[87]. Although it seemed to be a relatively simple campaign compared to the one in Parthia, which had required imperial forces to confront the most fearful cavalry units of that time, it turned out to be more difficult than anticipated. The legionaries were under continuous attacks from the Caledonians and Maeatae[88], and had immense difficulty penetrating the rugged Scottish Lowlands. Roman success was fleeting here. The territorial acquisitions, obtained by suffering considerable losses, were abandoned by Septimius' son Caracalla upon his death in 211[89].

---

[84] Zosimus, *New History*, 1, 8, 2.

[85] D. Oates, "The Roman Frontier in Northern Iraq", *The Geographical Journal*, Vol. 122, No. 2 (Jun., 1956), pp. 194-195. Also see M. H. Dodgeon and S.N.C. Lieu, *The Roman Eastern Frontier and the Persian Wars (AD 226-363)*.

[86] Cassius Dio, *Roman History*, 76, 11.

[87] Ibidem, 77, 11.

[88] Ibidem, 77, 13, 2.

[89] N. Hodgson, "The British Expedition of Septimius Severus", *Britannia*, Society for the Promotion of Roman Studies, Vol. 45 (2014), pp. 31-51.

The new emperor immediately distinguished himself as a brutal and bloodthirsty successor, killing his brother Geta to remain in power alone. Shortly after, he made a large donation of 2,500 *denarii* to the Praetorian Guard to secure their support[90]. In order to continue his father's policy of substantially funding the army, Caracalla enacted a new monetary reform which further devalued the *denarius* (it went from being 55% silver at the beginning of his reign to 51% at the time of his death)[91]. From then on, the relationship between *aurei* and *denarii* became increasingly distorted (in theory, 1 *aureus* was meant to be equivalent to 25 *denarii* but during the Severian Age, much more money was required to match the value of an *aureo*, given the damage done to the currency over the years by certain emperors). First, the weight of the *aureus* decreased from 7.2 to 6.5 grams then a new coin was introduced, which historians called the *antoninianus*[92], supposedly valuing two *denarii*.

Although it is possible that the original intention was to restore the monetary system, Caracalla's reform failed, partly because the new currency was actually worth 1.5 *denarii* (and not two) and partly because the *antoninianus* was withdrawn immediately after the death of the emperor[93]. The consequences were terrible for Rome. This marked the beginning of uncontrollable inflation.

"At the beginning, the devaluation undoubtedly provided the state with good results. Nevertheless, over the years, this device was abused and the century of inflation caused great damage to state finances. Prices grew too fast and it was impossible to rely on an immediate and proportional increase in tax revenues, given the rigidity of the tax collection system.[94]"

---

[90] Herodian, *History of the Roman Empire Since the Death of Marcus Aurelius*, 4, 4, 7.

[91] K. Butcher, *Debasement and the Decline of Rome*, pp. 182-201, part of R. Bland, D. Calomino, *Studies in Ancient Coinage in Honour of Andrew Burnett*, Spink & Son Ltd, London, 2015.

[92] Ibidem.

[93] Ibidem.

[94] A. Bernardi, *The Economic Problems of the Roman Empire at the Time of Its Decline*, Pontificia Universitas Lateranensis, Rome, 1965, p. 39.

The negative outcome of these measures is best captured by Gresham's Law which dictates that "bad money drives out good". The empire's inhabitants began to hoard *denarii* with higher silver content while at the same time using *denarii* with less worth in the market to pay for goods. Thanks to the *Constitutio Antoniniana*, a provision which granted Roman citizenship (and the tax burdens that went along with it) to all the inhabitants of the empire, Septimius's son met his short-term objectives despite the devaluation of the *denarius*. New revenue allowed him to increase legionary pay by 50% (which at its peak reached 900 *denarii*)[95]. Once the army was properly bankrolled, Caracalla moved towards the East to conquer Parthia. His goal was to succeed where his father had failed, following in the footsteps of his great idol, Alexander the Great[96].

The Romans penetrated deeply into Asian territory during this campaign, sacking Arbela and profaning the tombs of the Parthian sovereigns, even going so far as to trespass in Media (today's Iran)[97]; however, no decisive confrontation took place with the enemy and therefore, the success that they had was only temporary. Roman ambitions aggravated a serious crisis in the Parthian Empire: continuous Roman pummelling had undermined the credibility of the ruling Arsacid dynasty. After a bloody civil war, the dynasty was overthrown by Ardashir I, the forefather of the Persian Sasanian dynasty[98]. This handover involved innumerable changes in the eastern region. First, the new rulers of the Iranian plateau were driven by a strong ideological motivation[99]. They adhered to a unique religion (Zoroastrianism) with imperialistic underpinnings, which portrayed the Sassanids as inheritors of the legacy left by the great Persian conquerors of the past.

---

[95] P.I. Prodromidis, *Another View on an Old Inflation: Environment and Policies in the Roman Empire up to Diocletian's Price Edict*, Centre of Planning and Economic Research, Athens, February 2006, p. 13.

[96] Herodian, *History of the Roman Empire Since the Death of Marcus Aurelius*, 4, 8, 1.

[97] Historia Augusta, *Caracalla*, 6, 4.

[98] Cassius Dio, *Roman History*, 80, 3, 1-2.

[99] E. Luttwak, *The Grand Strategy of the Roman Empire* (1976), Bur Rizzoli, 2016, p. 278.

The strong centralization of their state and its efficient bureaucracy abetted their ambitions. But what the Romans had to fear the most were the improvements made by the Sassanids to the Persian war machine. Unlike the Parthian army, which was based on the manoeuvrability of archers on horseback, the new dynasty set about creating a military force based entirely on armoured heavy cavalry, called at the time, cataphract cavalry.

"Moreover, all the companies were clad in iron, and all parts of their bodies were covered with thick plates, so fitted that the stiff joints conformed with those of their limbs; and the forms of human faces were so skilfully fitted to their heads, that, since their entire bodies were plated with metal, arrows that fell upon them could lodge only where they could see a little through tiny openings fitted to the circle of the eye, or where through the tips of their noses they were able to get a little breath.[100]"

These *ante litteram* tanks, despite constituting a serious threat to the legionaries (as we will see later), were not considered novel at the time. In fact, the Sassanids augmented their already potent offensive with a tactic never fully grasped by the Parthians: the art of siege[101]. Soon after, rams and catapults became a constant threat to all cities in the East[102]. It was clear that the Romans from then on would no longer be facing a regional force of modest size (as was the nation ruled by the Arsacids), but a real imperial power, with an organized army and with expansionist aims that reached as far as the Aegean [103] . The transformation of the external threats to the empire did not only concern the East. Under Caracalla, the Alemanni invaded Roman territory for the first time[104].

[100] Ammianus Marcellinus, *History*, 25, 1, 12.
[101] Cassius Dio, *Roman History*, 80, 3, 3.
[102] E. Luttwak, *The Grand Strategy of the Roman Empire* (1976), Bur Rizzoli, 2016, p. 278-279.
[103] Herodian, *History of the Roman Empire Since the Death of Marcus Aurelius*, 6, 2, 2.
[104] Cassius Dio, *Roman History*, 78, 13, 4.

This episode is worthy of mention not so much for the damage inflicted, given that the barbarians were massacred by a single legion in short order, but because it was a fuller manifestation of something that had first occurred with the fall of the Marcomanni in 170. Unlike the disorderly mob led by Ballomar, the Alemanni were a consolidated league of various peoples (it is no coincidence that the word Alemanni quite likely means "all men[105]") that lived close to the Roman provinces of Raetia and Germania Superior[106].

Depiction of a Sassanid cataphract knight from Taq-e Bostan, Iran.

---

[105] H.J. Hummer, "The Fluidity of Barbarian Identity: The Ethnogenesis of Alemanni and Suebi, AD 200-500", *Early Medieval Europe*, 1998, Blackwell Publishers Ltd, Oxford, 7 (1), p. 4.

[106] Ibidem, pp. 1–27.

The *barbaricum*'s ethnography described more than a century before by Tacitus [107] consisted of minor tribes often hostile to each other. Nonetheless, there was an opportunity to form a confederation of different peoples united by their common interests. If, during Caracalla's reign, Rome's main adversaries were growing stronger, it was under the last ruler of the Severan dynasty, Alexander, that they became truly threatening. The young emperor immediately found himself having to check the expansionism of Ardashir I who, after a few years of solidifying his position, crossed the Tigris and claimed all the territories from Mesopotamia to the Propontis[108]. The Persians quickly advanced to the Euphrates River, but failed to conquer any of the Roman fortresses in the region. After assessing the situation, Alexander divided the twelve legions he had available into three large armies: one would march north through the Armenian mountains to reach Media; one would head south to the Euphrates River; and the central army, led by the emperor himself, would pass through Khabur-Singara in order to break through Persian lines in Mesopotamia and conquer Ctesiphon[109]. Historical information about the outcome of the campaign is not conclusive. It is probable that only the central Roman army was successful, driving the invaders back to the Tigris. However, to the south, the Romans were swept away by the bulk of the Persian forces, while to the north the legions suffered numerous casualties due to cold temperatures and lack of adequate equipment[110]. It was therefore a limited strategic victory, since Rome returned to its pre-war borders. Still, maintaining the status quo came at a cost.

"A great many soldiers suffered mutilation in the frigid country, and only a handful of the large number of troops who started the march managed to reach Antioch. The emperor led his own large force to that city, and many of them perished too; so, the affair brought the greatest discontent to the army and the greatest dishonour to

---

[107] This refers to the work "Germania" by the Roman historian Tacitus, which was an ethnographic treatment of the populations that lived beyond the Rhine during Antiquity.

[108] Herodian, *History of the Roman Empire Since the Death of Marcus Aurelius*, 6, 2-5.

[109] Ibidem, 6, 5, 1.

[110] Ibidem, 6, 5, 5-9.

Alexander, who was betrayed by bad luck and bad judgment. Of the three armies into which he had divided his total force, the greater part was lost by various misfortunes - disease, war, and cold.[111]"

Returning from the East, Alexander had to face a new wave of attacks on the Germanic limes, which was exactly what had happened to Marcus Aurelius a few decades earlier[112]. The Alemanni had invaded Noricum, Rezia and Germania Superior, this time inflicting serious damage to important urban centres such as Castra Regina and Augusta Treverorum. The legions succeeded in blocking the invaders but instead of counterattacking, the emperor decided to strike a deal with the barbarians, offering them money in exchange for a truce. Roman soldiers, already demoralized by serious losses suffered in Mesopotamia, regarded this submissive gesture with outrage and decided to mutiny[113]. Alexander Severus was executed by a number of legionaries within military quarters at Mogontiacum in 235.

Near collapse

It was the successor of Alexander Severus, Maximinus Thrax, who inaugurated a period that is typically referred to as the "Crisis of the Third Century". A general of very humble origins[114], he immediately antagonized the senatorial aristocracy, instead attaching imperial authority to military power. Maximinus immediately saw to solidifying his position by increasing the pay of the legionaries (who received between 1,200 and 1,800 *denarii* per year[115]). Then he organized an expedition to punish the Alemanni.

---

[111] Ibidem, 6, 6, 3.

[112] Ibidem, 7, 1, 6.

[113] Ibidem.

[114] Eutropius, *Breviarium ab Urbe condita*, 9, 1.

[115] P.I. Prodromídis, *Another View on an Old Inflation: Environment and Policies in the Roman Empire up to Diocletian's Price Edict*, Centre of Planning and Economic Research, Athens, February 2006, p.13.

The Roman army surged hundreds of kilometres into Germanic territory[116], going as far as where Lower Saxony is today. Recent archaeological findings have shown that a great battle took place between the Romans and the barbarians in an area that, after the Battle of the Teutoburg Forest, was thought to be completely out of imperial range[117].

Maximinus returned victorious from his expedition in Germany and then travelled to the Danube where he pacified the Iazyges, Dacians, Quadi and even the Goths. The emperor's military ambitions went beyond simply deterring possible invaders. Maximinus wanted to emulate Marcus Aurelius and effectively extend control over Magna Germany[118]. However, the ongoing wars that Rome had waged had drained the empire and were becoming unsustainable.

"It was thus possible every day to see men who yesterday had been rich, today reduced to paupers, so great was the avarice of the tyrant, who pretended to be insuring a continuous supply of money for the soldiers. (...) After Maximinus had impoverished most of the distinguished men and confiscated their estates, which he considered small and insignificant and not sufficient for his purposes, he turned to the public treasuries; all the funds which had been collected for the citizens' welfare or for gifts, all the funds being held in reserve for shows or festivals, he transferred to his own personal fortune. The offerings which belonged to the temples, the statues of the gods, the tokens of honour of the heroes, the decorations on public buildings, the adornments of the city, in short, any material suitable for making coins, he handed over to the mints. (...) But what especially irked the people and aroused public indignation was the fact that, although no fighting was going on and no enemy was under arms anywhere, Rome appeared to be a city under siege.[119]"

To fund his military ambitions, Maximinus had implemented a policy of "direct appropriation" of taxes and supplies, which often resulted in real terrorism.

---

[116] Aurelius Victor, *De Caesaribus*, 26, 1.

[117] This refers to the Battle at the Harzhorn, which involved thousands of barbarian and Roman soldiers. Discovered in 2008, the site of the battle was a marvel to historians. To read more: U. Livadiotti, Herodian (7, 2, 1-8), *le megistai eikones di Massimino e la guerra germanica del 235*, Thiasos, 4, 2015, pp. 109-122.

[118] Historia Augusta, *The Two Maximini*, 11-12.

[119] Herodian, *History of the Roman Empire Since the Death of Marcus Aurelius*, 7, 3, 3-6.

This *modus operandi* was not tolerated for long by the Roman people and at the beginning of 238 a great revolt broke out in North Africa provoked by the emperor's extortions[120]. The Gordian family, who led the uprising, occupied Carthage and subsequently named two of its most distinguished members, Gordian I and Gordian II, as co-emperors. As soon as Maximinus learned that the riots had also swallowed up the capital, he decided to lead his army to the Italian peninsula[121].

The events that followed were rather chaotic: the two Gordians were killed in Africa by troops loyal to Maximinus and the Senate quickly decided to elect two new *Augusti*, Marcus Clodius Pupienus Maximus Augustus and Decimus Caelius Calvinus Balbinus[122]. Meanwhile Maximinus steadily advanced to Aquileia and besieged the city although his troops did not vanquish it[123]. The city put up a tenacious defense while several senatorial contingents approached and food supplies for the Roman army ran low. As a result, the soldiers lost confidence in the emperor who, abandoned by the entire civilian population, was eventually killed by his own men in May of 238[124]. In the capital uprisings continued to rage resulting in the fall of both Pupienus and Balbinus. Eventually, Gordian III, grandson of Gordian I, was installed by the Praetorian Guard. The wild vicissitudes of the empire had not gone unnoticed. In the East, first Ardashir and then his son Shapur had taken advantage of Roman infighting to penetrate the province of Mesopotamia and seize the cities of Hatra, Nisibis and Carrhae[125]. Gordian III left immediately for Syria where, with the vital support of his father-in-law (and praetorian prefect) Timesitheus, he prepared to launch a counter-offensive against the Persians.

---

[120] Historia Augusta, *The Two Maximini*, 13-14.
[121] Ibidem, 20, 1.
[122] Ibidem.
[123] Ibidem, 22, 4-7.
[124] Zosimus, *New History*, 1, 15, 1-2.
[125] Zonaras, *Extracts of History*, 12, 18.

The initial military operations favoured the Romans, who reoccupied Carrhae, Nisibis and Singara and overwhelmed the Sassanids in the Battle of Resaena[126]. However, the sudden death of Timesitheus, the true commander of the Roman expeditionary force, changed everything: the Persians took advantage of the young emperor's inexperience and won decisively at the Battle of Mesiche (near today's Fallujah). Despite the propaganda circulated by Shapur I, who wanted people to believe that the emperor had died at the battle, Gordian probably died at the hands of his successor, Marcus Julius Philippus Augustus or from wounds sustained in a fall from a horse[127]. In the end, the Persians only claimed the city of Hatra and avoided clashing with the Romans for almost a decade. For the time being, there was relative quiet in the East (Armenia had been abandoned and the Sassanids appeased with about 500,000 denarii[128]). The new emperor Philip the Arab hastened to Rome to stabilize his position then headed to the Danube, where Roman forces had to repel the Quadi and Carpi. But it was the Goths who created the most problems for the emperor[129]. These were people originally from southern Sweden who were made *foederati* (allies of Rome living beyond the border but charged with defending the empire from possible invaders). This pact was signed during the reign of Gordian III and the Goths subsequently participated in his campaign against the Persians. Unfortunately, Philip did not grant the annual sum of money that the pact had guaranteed (most likely because more taxes would have caused further unrest in Rome after the money raised to appease Shapur) and the Goths decided to break the alliance by invading the empire[130]. The barbarians devastated Thrace and Lower Moesia before being stopped by imperial troops near Marcianopolis.

---

[126] Eutropius, *Breviarium ab Urbe condita*, 9, 2.

[127] Ibidem.

[128] L. de Blois, *The Reign of Emperor Philp the Arabian*, Free University, Amsterdam, 1978, p. 14.

[129] For more information on the Goths and their impact on the Empire: I. Nordgren, *The Well Spring of the Goths: About the Gothic Peoples in the Nordic Countries and on the Continent*, iUniverse, Inc. New York Lincoln Shanghai, 2004.

[130] Jordanes, *De origine actibusque Getarum*, 16, 1-3.

Philip's fortunes began to decline due to further devaluation of the currency, a pernicious trend since Septimius Severus had first debased the *denarius*. The soldiers wanted higher wages, given the rising prices of goods caused by inflation, but the imperial coffers were empty. The wars on the Danube, tributes to the Persians and barbarians, riches bestowed upon the troops at the beginning of his reign and other significant expenses prevented the emperor from satisfying the army's requests[131]. It was for this reason that the legions decided to acclaim a new emperor, named Decius, who defeated the Arab near Verona[132].

Although he was judged harshly by history, Philip showed himself to have the qualities of a good emperor, with respect to his dealings with the Senate and management of the border war[133]. Moreover, like Severus Alexander, he would have been considered a more successful ruler if he had lived in more prosperous times or when the Augustan model of traditional authority still existed. But the times in which he lived necessitated urgent changes, which Philip never fully delivered[134]. As aforementioned, his successor was Decius, a general of Illyrian origin. Decius, also known as Trajan Decius, was an appreciator of the former glory of imperial Rome. He proposed changes to the judiciaries, initiated the construction of new public works and promoted the Roman religion. He was named *optimus princeps* by the Senate[135]. New invasions from the North soon forced him to leave the Italian peninsula. During the winter of 250, a hoard of Goths, taking advantage of the frozen Danube, poured into what is today Bulgaria, defeating the imperial army and looting the city of Philippopolis. Despite the raids, the following year the barbarians were quelled by Decius. Defeated, they offered to give back loot and prisoners in exchange for an undisturbed return beyond the Danube.

---

[131] L. de Blois, *The Reign of Emperor Philp the Arabian*, Free University, Amsterdam, 1978, p. 41-43.

[132] Eutropius, *Breviarium ab Urbe condita*, 9, 3.

[133] Ibidem.

[134] Ibidem.

[135] Ibidem, 9, 4.

Surprisingly, the emperor, in a lapse of judgment, not only refused the proposed agreement, but also decided to attack the retreating Goths. Fought in the Dobruja, the battle was an utter catastrophe for the empire. Both Decius and his son died in the conflict[136]. The new emperor Trebonianus Gallus appeased the Goths, granting them permission to keep their booty inside Roman territory and also promising them lavish gifts in the future[137]. Decius' successor turned out to be incapable of handling the problems besetting the empire. He did little to prevent the sudden return of the Goths to imperial territory, who ravaged the coasts of the Black Sea and the Aegean, reaching the city of Ephesus (in present-day Turkey). But the most serious threat to Rome was still from the East. Shapur, taking advantage of the political chaos riddling the West, launched a violent offensive against the Roman defenses of the Euphrates at the beginning of 253. The Persians conquered the stronghold of Nisibis, defeated the eastern legions near Barbalissos, and then continued to penetrate Licaonia, Cappadocia and Syria, finally conquering Antioch[138].

The Roman response came only when, after the death of two other emperors, Publius Licinius Valerian came to power. After putting his son Gallienus in charge of the western part of the empire, the new emperor headed east, and immediately retook Antioch. Here, despite the destruction of the Roman fortress of Dura Europos, the legions succeeded in driving the Persians back to Mesopotamia. In the West, Gallienus had to cope with new aggressions from the Goths, who had become more skilled at laying siege and acquired an impressive fleet. They successfully sacked the Balkans and various Black Sea cities[139]. For this reason, Valerian decided to send a contingent to defend Byzantium and the Bosphoros, vital for the supply of wheat to the empire[140]. The Goth raids required decisive action but the East once again undercut imperial plans.

---

[136] Jordanes, *De origine actibusque Getarum*, 18, 3.
[137] Zosimus, *New History*, 1, 24, 2.
[138] Eutropius, *Breviarium ab Urbe condita*, 9, 8 and Zosimo, *Storia nuova*, 1, 27, 2.
[139] Ibidem, 1, 29-33.
[140] Historia Augusta, *Aurelian*, 13, 2.

The Sassanids became hostile again in 260 and Valerian had to immediately return to the East, where the Roman army, weakened by the plague, was wiped out by the Persians near Edessa. The emperor himself fell into enemy hands[141]. This great victory allowed Shapur to invade Syria and Cappadocia, retaking Antioch[142].

Rome had not found itself in such difficulty since the time of the Punic Wars. The empire had been internally weakened by inflation, which increased prices and compelled Roman rulers to institute oppressive taxes. Strife within the empire had made the stability that had characterized most of its first two centuries utterly impossible. Moreover, Rome's adversaries were undoubtedly more formidable than those faced in the past. Upon the death of his father, Gallienus found himself with an empire in shambles, not on strong footing in the East and defenseless to the incursions of the Goths. It was from this nadir, *paradoxically*, that the empire began to rise again.

---

[141] Aurelius Victor, *De Caesaribus*, 32, 5.
[142] Agathias Scholasticus, *On the Reign of Justinian*, 4, 24, 3.

Third Chapter

The Resurgence of Rome

Strategic and territorial reorganization

"The Resurgence of Rome" was a slow and painful process that lasted about forty years and was not without struggles along the way. It was finally realized under Diocletian, who dragged the empire out of instability. Although many identify the beginning of Rome's revival as the reign of Aurelian during the third century, it would be a mistake not to mention the fundamental contribution of Gallienus to its rehabilitation. In fact, Gallienus implemented numerous policies that not only revolutionized the imperial approach towards its various external commitments, but also changed Roman society from within, making it possible for individuals like Aurelian and Diocletian himself to acquire power. Perhaps he was motivated by the cruel fate of his father Valerian to bring into effect the first significant changes to the workings of the imperial machine. For this reason, we will use him as a starting point from which to examine Rome's response to this devastating crisis.

Redrawing the Empire

Under Gallienus the first measures were taken to withdraw from the most expensive regions in economic and military terms, which involved Agri Decumates and Dacia. The first region to be withdrawn from was tucked between the Rhine and Danube Rivers and bounded by the

Swabian Alps, Black Forest and the River Main. This region was gradually occupied by Vespasian and then by Domitian between A.D. 70 and A.D. 90[143]. Their conquests made it possible to build a new frontier made of artificial fortifications between the Taunus mountain range and the Wetterau plains[144].

The Agri Decumates constituted a strategic point made of artificial defenses
that needed to be constantly manned by numerous soldiers.
The black dots represent the auxiliary forts and
the squares, the castra legionaries.

---

[143] "Frontiers of the Roman Empire", *whc.unesco.org*, (retrieved February 15, 2018).
[144] Ibidem.

This fortification was enlarged by Trajan, who built the Odenwald Limes, and Hadrian, who added a new line on the Alb River. The entire border was further consolidated by Antoninus Pius, who had several stone fortifications built[145]. The new limes were undoubtedly a better alternative to the natural defenses offered by the Rhine and Danube. They defended lands that lent themselves well to agriculture and were therefore, possible sites for civilization[146]. The region, merged with the province of Germania Superior, was populated by Romanized Gauls and was prosperous at least until the beginning of the third century when the Alemanni began raiding it. However, the situation grew more volatile during the reigns of Alexander Severus and Maximinus Thrax, and eventually became intolerable in the days of Valerian[147]. The problem was that the Upper Germanic-Rhaetian Limes were unsustainable for the economy because of the Roman troops required: 550 km of frontier, 60 *castella* [148] and 900 guard towers constituted a dense defensive network that relied on a considerable military garrison that had to be permanently stationed in order to function effectively[149]. Gallienus decided in 259 to withdraw from the region and rebuild the defenses along the Danube-Iller-Reno line, a border that already existed before the Germanic campaigns of Vespasian and his son Domitian[150]. This choice probably made the Romans less effective in the region from a strategic standpoint; however, it was much easier to defend since fewer troops were needed to guard the naturally occurring borders, thus leaving some of the auxiliary units in the Agri Decumates available to be stationed elsewhere. Yet the area was only occupied for a short time by the emperor Aurelian and was immediately abandoned by his successor Probus.

---

[145] Ibidem.

[146] E. Luttwak, *The Grand Strategy of the Roman Empire* (1976), Bur Rizzoli, 2016, p. 174-178.

[147] J. G. F. Hind, "Whatever Happened to the 'Agri Decumates'?", *Britannia*, Society for the Promotion of Roman Studies, Vol. 15 (1984), pp. 187-192.

[148] The *castella* were forts used for stationing small detachments of troops.

[149] E. Luttwak, *The Grand Strategy of the Roman Empire* (1976), Bur Rizzoli, 2016, p. 178.

[150] J. G. F. Hind, "Whatever Happened to the 'Agri Decumates'?", *Britannia*, Society for the Promotion of Roman Studies, Vol. 15 (1984), pp. 189-192.

It was clear that Rome could no longer control a completely artificial border[151].

Dacia had to be carefully considered. Its inhabitants had been a menace since the time of Julius Caesar[152]; firstly, because they were fearsome warriors and secondly, because they possessed many precious metals, which made them almost immune to Roman "diplomatic proposals". Domitian tried to annex the region through a series of invasions but his efforts proved unsuccessful[153]. Taking the opportunity to avenge Domitian's defeat, the emperor Trajan personally commanded an expedition against the Dacians which, after five years of war, resulted in the Romans occupying the region. The reasons for the conquest only partly concerned Roman honour: Trajan lusted after Dacia's gold and silver mines which could have alone filled the imperial coffers for several decades. Furthermore, there was the need to adopt a new strategy in the region. The Danube was seen as a unified front beyond which lurked innumerable threats for the empire. If, together with the Dacians, they had decided to attack the Marcomanni, Quadi and Sarmatians, Rome could not have defended itself adequately[154]. On one hand, the new Roman province of Dacia guaranteed a generous economic return (not counting the revenue from the mines, it is said that the spoils of the Dacian campaign amounted to 163.6 tons of gold and about twice that of silver[155]). On the other hand, it represented a strong *ultra flumen* outpost, providing Roman troops with the opportunity for tactical (and diplomatic) manoeuvres that were critical for controlling the area.

---

[151] Ibidem.

[152] Appian, *The Civil Wars*, 2, 111. The famous Roman leader was preparing an expedition to punish the Dacian king Burebista, who had supported Pompey in the civil war. However, he was assassinated shortly before departure during the infamous Ides of March.

[153] Cassius Dio, *Roman History*, 68, 9, 3.

[154] E. Luttwak, *The Grand Strategy of the Roman Empire* (1976), Bur Rizzoli, 2016, p. 185-189.

[155] Cassius Dio, *Roman History*, 58, 14, 4-5.

Yet this only made sense if the overall structure on which it rested remained strong and functional.

"The military worth of an outpost declines and finally becomes a liability as the security on the baseline diminishes. Thus, in the great crisis of the third century, when Rome lost control of the Sarmatians on either side of the salient, the *Limes Porolissensis* did become a vulnerable salient liable to be cut off, as well as a drain on the resources of the sector as a whole.[156]"

Dacia was one of the areas of the empire richest in precious metals.
However, its defense became unsustainable in the third century.
As many as 50,000 soldiers guarded it during this period.
Potaissa and Apulum, basecamps with two legions, are highlighted.

---

[156] E. Luttwak, *The Grand Strategy of the Roman Empire* (1976), Bur Rizzoli, 2016, p. 190.

Starting from the reign of Gordian III, the entire region was targeted by Carpi raiders and specifically the Goths, a new and intense threat around the Danube[157]. The threat increased with time, provoking Philip the Arab to gather troops from Upper Moesia, Germania Superior and other provinces in order to defend the southern part of Dacia, which was fragile and exposed[158]. Since Decius' death in battle, the situation in the region had worsened. The hordes of Carpi and Goths moved from the plains of Bessarabia, Moldavia and Wallachia and then descended upon the Roman provinces of Moesia and Thrace. It is no coincidence that cities like Sucidava and Romula (in southern Dacia) had their interiors fortified, at great cost[159]. By contrast, the Roman borders in the north served their purpose despite the fact that no city was similarly fortified[160]. The problem was that the barbarian incursions cut off several kilometres of limes, making the two legions at the garrison in northern Dacia virtually useless.

"The defensive system of Dacia was largely conceived and organized under Trajan and fully developed in the reign of Hadrian. Very few changes were made later. Hadrian's successors improved the defensive system only in detail (...). The later territorial changes did not alter the principles on which the *limes* were organized. It appears that the defensive system reached its maximum strength at the beginning of the third century in the time of the Severi, when the majority of the forts was built in stone and the total of military units was at its greatest. The withdrawal from Dacia in 275 was not due to the weakness or the destruction of the Dacian defensive but rather to the events that occurred outside Dacia, especially to the disasters in Moesia Inferior and Thracia. By then the defense system of Dacia could only protect Dacia; its strength could no longer contribute to the defense of neighbouring provinces. Its role was outdated.[161]"

---

[157] Ibidem.

[158] D. Tudor, "The Fortification of Roman Cities in Dacia in the Third Century", *Historia: Zeitschrift für Alte Geschichte*, Franz Steiner Verlag, Bd. 14, H. 3 (Jul., 1965), p. 370.

[159] Ibidem, pp. 377-379.

[160] Ibidem.

[161] N. Gudea, "The Defensive System of Roman Dacia", *Britannia*, Society for the Promotion of Roman Studies, Vol. 10 (1979), p. 66.

The colossal Dacian defensive system was a folly for the Roman Empire of the third century. At the beginning of the reign of Gallienus, the province was garrisoned by two legions, the XIII *Gemina* stationed at Apulum and the V *Macedonica* at Potaissa. Almost 40,000 units of auxiliary troops were added to these, including *alae, numeri, coohortes miliarie* and *quingenarie*[162]. More than 50,000 men[163] (more than one tenth of the total Roman troops) defended Dacia alone. Rome could not afford that number of men even during what was an acute crisis. Gallienus commanded troops to abandon southern Dacia in 256 and subsequently, Aurelian, between 271 and 275, carried out *amissio Daciae*, evacuating all the Roman colonists on this side of the Danube[164].

Further lands were reconciled thanks to the stability guaranteed during the Period of the Tetrarchy (284-305). In this case, the regions concerned were located on the other side of the Mediterranean, in the African provinces controlled by the Romans. The security of the southern *limes* had been undermined by the imperial government's neglect, which had increasingly encouraged the action of local raiders[165]. The first area to be reconciled was Egypt which had been a granary of Rome since the early days of the Republic. It was always subjected to strict control by emperors. In addition to the cereals that the banks of the Nile periodically provided, the region was a very important commercial intersection for sub-Saharan Africa and the Far East. Rome obtained precious metals, slaves, ivory, beasts for *ludi* and other luxury goods in exchanges made here[166]. For this reason, the warlike activity of the Nubian tribes could not be tolerated.

---

[162] *Ibidem*, pp. 65-66.
[163] P.L. MacKendrick, *The Dacian Stones Speak*, The University of North Carolina Press, 2000, p. 107 and I.A. Oltean, *Dacia: Landscape, Colonisation and Romanisation*, Routledge, 2007, p. 56.
[164] D. Tudor, "The Fortification of Roman Cities in Dacia in the Third Century", *Historia: Zeitschrift für Alte Geschichte*, Franz Steiner Verlag, Bd. 14, H. 3 (Jul., 1965), p. 380.
[165] Historia Augusta, *Probus*, 9, 1.
[166] R.B. Jackson, *At Empire's Edge. Exploring Rome's Egyptian Frontier*. 2002, p. 86.

Diocletian, who went as far as Elephantine in 298, decided to reorganize Egypt, which had remained practically untouched since the time of Augustus [167]. The southern border would have played an important role in this reorganization. The *aethiopicus* border was moved to the North, from Hyerasykaminos (Maharraqah) to Philae (File), near the First Cataract. The territory of Dodecaschoenus was thus cut off and difficult to defend, making it now easy prey for Blemmyes raids [168]. The emperor did not completely abandon that territory. Instead, he simply decided that direct control over an area so poor and extensive was too great a burden. He conferred the status *foederati* upon the Nile people the Nobates, who settled in the territories left by the Roman troops and agreed to defend the territory against the Blemmyes. With the troops "acquired" through territorial retrenchment, a new and intelligent defense system was created, which was much more focused on the protection of the Nile valley. Adding to the already numerous camel and cavalry *alae*, the emperor created the I *Maximiana*, which was stationed right in Philae [169]. To complement the new order, Diocletian commissioned the construction of many military works. The main fortifications were located east of the Nile, between Coptos (Qift) and Kaine (Qena), but also to the west in the area of the *Oasi Magna*, near Dahkla and the Kharga Oasis [170].

---

[167] Procopius, *History of the Wars*, 1, 19.

[168] L. P. Kirwan, "Rome beyond the Southern Egyptian Frontier", *The Geographical Journal*, Vol. 123, No. 1 (Mar., 1957), pp. 13-19.

[169] "Legio I Maximiana", *livius.org*, (retrieved February 16, 2018).

[170] A.L. Boozer, "Frontiers and Borderlands in Imperial Perspectives: Exploring Rome's Egyptian Frontier", *American Journal of Archaeology*, Archaeological Institute of America, Vol. 117, No. 2 (April 2013), pp. 275-292.

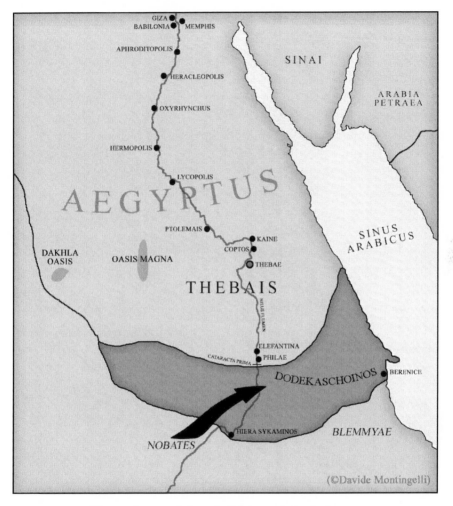

The territory ceded to the Nobates is in dark gray.
Diocletian entrusted much of the burden of the Egyptian defense to the allies
during this operation.

From archaeological evidence we see that many of the forts were designed simply as deterrents since they could not withstand serious and coordinated attacks. This was intentional. Roman engineers built them in direct response to the needs that that specific sector presented[171]. The threat posed by the Nubian tribes was certainly sporadic rather than endemic like that of the Danubian tribes.

The reorganization also included the central part of northern Africa. Here, starting from the Trajan Age, the Romans had gone further and further into the interior, in order to remove the indigenous marauders from the great Roman cities such as Carthage and Leptis Magna[172]. Septimius Severus took particular care of his place of birth. Under his reign the Roman troops defeated the Garamantes, a desert population that raided the Libyan coast, occupying their capital Garama for a short period of time[173]. One of the architects of the victory, Quintus Anicius Faustus, took the opportunity to create a deep defensive salient in Libyan territory, based on the model in the Dacian provinces. The strategy behind this territorial foothold was as simple as it was effective. The raiders needed to store water because their bases were located far away from the coastal cities, so the Romans created forts to police all the major oases in the area in order to make offensive initiatives logistically difficult[174]. The fortifications built at Gadames, Gheriat el-Garbia and Goliath definitively consolidated the *limes tripolitanus*[175]. During the tumult of the third century, the area was abandoned, left to fate. The only legion that still had a presence there, the III *Augusta*, was finally discharged by Gordian III[176].

It was only under Diocletian that the area was reorganized.

---

[171] Ibidem.

[172] S. Rinaldi Tufi, *Archeologia delle Province Romane*, Rome, 2007, p. 380.

[173] J.S. Wacher, *The Roman World*, Taylor and Francis, Vol.1, 2002, pp. 252-253.

[174] "Limes Tripolitanus", *livius.org*, (retrieved February 17, 2018).

[175] R. G. Goodchild and J. B. Ward Perkins, "The Limes Tripolitanus in the Light of Recent Discoveries", *The Journal of Roman Studies*, Society for the Promotion of Roman Studies, Vol. 39, Parts 1 and 2 (1949), pp. 81-95.

[176] "Limes Tripolitanus", *livius.org*, (retrieved February 17, 2018).

The salient disappeared and the limes became the entire defense for the *centenaria*, fortified farms protected by armed peasants[177]. It was a much less expensive solution than that of a "formal" defense consisting of legions and auxiliary units, and one that, in some ways, anticipated the appearance of the *limitanei*.

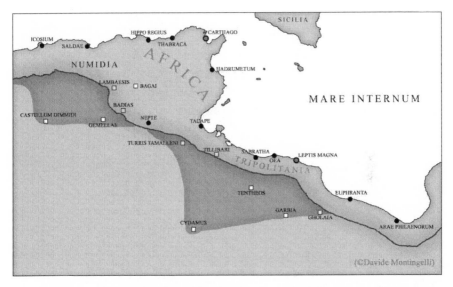

The territories abandoned by the Romans after changes made to the North African border are in dark gray.

The last territory to be subjected to a withdrawal was Mauritania, located in North Africa's western extremity. Beginning in 297, the Emperor Maximian successfully conducted several military operations in this area against the Berber tribes that were attacking Roman territories. The victories were regarded as opportunities to understand *how* to better defend the area and exactly what to defend within it. During the empire's first centuries, Mauritania was divided into two parts: the easternmost part was called *Mauretania Cesariensis*, while the westernmost was called *Mauretania Tingitana*.

---

[177] Ibidem.

The latter was the more problematic of the two. Once the settlements near the Atlantic were removed there was nothing to draw the semi-nomadic tribes from the interior who were simply not attracted by the comforts that Roman cities offered[178]; furthermore, the impervious terrain of the region favoured the guerrilla tactics used by the natives[179], who never fully recognized imperial authority. Although it had been annexed in A.D. 40, the region only prospered in areas defended by Roman garrisons, where the cities of Tingi, Lixus and Volubilis were located. As the decades passed, the failure of Romanization became evident. More and more often the populations from the interior struck Roman centres in Mauretania. Volubilis, in particular, was targeted by the Baquates tribe from Mauretania.

"First, Volubilis was not near the sea and easy communications and transport. In addition, the mountains to the south, west and east made it quite difficult for the Romans to defend the city from raiding mountain tribes. As for the Baquates, unlike the Autololes (another tribe from Mauretania), they could raid the city and easily take refuge in the mountains. Further, they may not have had the option, seemingly available to the Autololes, of finding grazing land elsewhere. When winter came, they had no choice but to bring their flocks down from the mountains. The supply of winter pasture land was limited and, no doubt, strictly allocated among tribes. The Baquates could not easily give up the land around Volubilis. Thus, the pressures put upon them by the Roman occupation may have been more intense than for the Autololes, and their resistance must have been more concerted.[180]"

---

[178] M. C. Sigman, "The Romans and the Indigenous Tribes of Mauretania Tingitana", *Historia: Zeitschrift für Alte Geschichte*, Franz Steiner Verlag, Bd. 26, H. 4 (4th Qtr., 1977), pp. 415-439.
[179] Ibidem.
[180] *Ibidem*, p. 431.

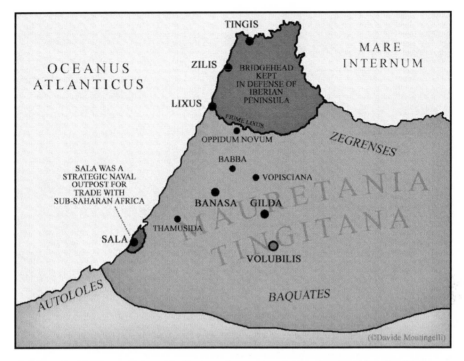

*Mauretania Tingitana: in dark gray the territories maintained by the Romans
following the reorganization by Maximian, in lighter gray
the abandoned territories and in italics the hostile tribes to the empire.
Also for strategic reasons the capital Volubilis was abandoned.*

The Romans tried several times to resolve the situation by military
and diplomatic means, but without obtaining lasting results. Finally,
given the great difficulty in establishing an effective military defense, it
was decided during the Tetrarchy that the settlements located closest to
the interior should be abandoned (with the exception of the coastal
centers of Sala and Mogador) thus bringing the border of the province
to the Lixus river[181]. The Romans thereby avoided what would have
been a reckless deployment of forces considering the relative poverty of
the area to defend. Fortifying a few strategic positions in the area of

---

[181] Ibidem, p. 434.

present-day Tangier, the empire created a solid bridgehead that guaranteed the possession of the Strait of Gibraltar and the consequent defense of *Hispania Baetica* from possible Berber incursions[182].

Maximian's redefinition of the borders was not painless for the region's economy, which lost substantial arable land[183]. Nevertheless, it was a strategic move consistent with the policy implemented by the tetrarchs in other parts of the imperial domain. The Romans would not intervene again in Mauretania until 429[184].

The beneficial secession of Palmyra and the Gauls

There is another important disengagement to be considered, one that was quite "unorthodox" but probably more decisive than those already mentioned; that is, the secession from the Gallic Empire in the West and the proclamation of the Kingdom of Palmyra in the East.

"Thus, while Gallienus abandoned the government, the Roman Empire was saved in the West by Posthumus, and in the East by Odenathus.[185]"

Despite the hatred shown by ancient historians to Gallienus (who also reproached him for the retreat from Dacia [186]), this passage from Eutropius underlines an important point; that is, how necessary it was for the Romans to avoid the enormous expenses that are normally involved in the direct control of a territory. The Gallic Empire was formed by Marcus Cassianius Latinius Postumus, governor of Germania Inferior and acclaimed by the troops in the Rhineland as *imperator* and undisputed ruler of Gaul, Britannia, Iberia and Germania[187].

---

[182] J. van Kuijck, *The Integration of Mauretania Tingitana in the Diocese of Hispaniae*, p. 9.
[183] Ibidem.
[184] Ibidem.
[185] Eutropius, *Breviarium ab Urbe condita*, 9, 11.
[186] Ibidem, 9, 8.
[187] Ibidem, 9, 9.

He established a veritable empire, which had not only its own capital (Cologne) but also a mint and a variety of institutions. Postumus fared well in foreign policy, too, decisively defeating the Franks and Alemanni. Although the independence of Gaul was in itself violent (Postumus had the praetorian prefect Silvanus and Gallienus's son Cornelius Saloninus killed), this secession significantly helped Rome to recovery from the Crisis of the Third Century.

This is ascertainable for many reasons: first of all, excluding two (understandable) attempts made by Gallienus to reconquer it, the Roman Empire and the Gallic Empire both repelled attacks by barbarian invaders in their respective areas of competence without battling each other; secondly, Postumus never did march towards Italy. It is not known whether his was a moral choice made in the name of *communis patria* or simply due to the fact that he could not leave the Rhine unguarded. Since his empire remained Roman in the traditional sense[188], the *imperator Galliarum* probably would have liked an official recognition from the capital. Furthermore, and this is a very unusual fact given how the Romans treated defeated usurpers, once the secessionist provinces were reattached in 274, Aurelian spared the life of the Gallic emperor[189]. Indeed, the emperor granted him an important civil office in southern Italy, and ensured that his subordinates in Gaul would maintain their roles in the reunited Roman Empire. None of the Gallic emperors were stricken from the annals, according to the custom of *damnatio memoriae*. Changes in Gaul were to be formally condemned by Rome, but Gallienus knew in his heart that they were necessary, given the continuous threats he had been facing on the Danube.

---

[188] M. Polfer, "Postumus (A.D. 260-269)", *roman-emperors.org*, (retrieved February 14, 2018).

[189] A. Goldsworthy, *How Rome Fell*, Yale University Press, 2009, p. 130

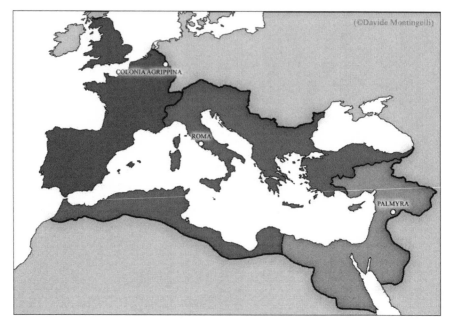

The "Tripartite" Empire: on the left the Gallic Empire, in the centre the Roman Empire and on the right the Kingdom of Palmyra.

The son of Valerian surely entertained the idea that one day he would be able to recover the western territories. But until then, the enormous territorial loss that Rome took actually allowed the empire to make substantial gains. In a few short years the empire had made these areas bear all the burdens of the defenses on the Rhine front and in Britain (ravaged by Saxon raids and piracy). With incredible discipline, Gallienus placed the needs of the empire before his personal desire to avenge his son, thereby favouring secession.

The same argument can be made for the political structure that was created in the East. After the death of Valerian in Edessa, the Romans were compelled to counterattack if they did not want to see Shapur parading through the streets of Byzantium. Septimius Odaenathus, a member of a prominent family in the Kingdom of Palmyra and also an individual who had received citizenship during the time of Septimius Severus, played a crucial role in changing the fortunes of the empire in the East. He joined the Romans in their efforts to expel the Sassanids from Syria and he openly sided with Gallienus against the attempted usurpation by a certain Macrianus. For his loyalty the emperor formally recognized his royal authority over all of Syria[190]. Odaenathus was not satisfied with these honours and in 262 he organized a great expedition against Shapur, which saw the reconquest of the lost territories, including Armenia and Mesopotamia, as well as the capture of Ctesiphon[191]. Gallienus rewarded the efforts of Odaenathus with the title of *corrector totius orientis*, which meant that the ruler of Palmyra was the *de facto* supreme commander of the Syrian legions and the regent of the eastern provinces of the Roman Empire. In this case the withdrawal from the commitment is less ambiguous than the one in the West, since Odaenathus was formally decorated by Rome and perhaps even named *Augustus* by the emperor[192]. Aurelian also continued the wise and necessary withdrawal policy initiated by Gallienus. When Vaballathus, son of the late Odaenathus, came to power, Rome quietly recognized him as the successor of his father in exchange for Zenobia (Vaballathus' mother) guaranteeing that Palmyra would protect Roman interests in the East. Proof of mutual recognition are coins minted in Antioch during this period, on which there are the head of Aurelian, bearded and wearing an imperial crown, and the head of Vaballathus, marked *vir clarissimus/consularis, rex, imperator* and *dux romanorum*[193]. The association was interrupted in 272, when the mint began to specify Zenobia's son as the only *Augustus* and therefore, legitimate Roman emperor. At this point Aurelian, who had meanwhile stabilized the situation in Italy and on the Danube, decided to march to annex the East.

---

[190] Historia Augusta, *The Two Gallieni*, 1-3.
[191] Zosimus, *New History*, 1, 39, 2.
[192] Historia Augusta, *The Two Gallieni*, 12, 1.
[193] A. Goldsworthy, *How Rome Fell*, Yale University Press, 2009, p. 127.

Roman coin which testifies to the "political condominium" in the East between Aurelian and Vaballathus.

After a series of three battles the emperor overcame Zenobia, regained the lost territories and earned the title of *Restaurator Orbis*. The fate of the rebel queen was similar to that of Tetricus. She was pardoned by Aurelian and was allowed to live near the capital and marry a Roman noble. As it follows, the secession of these two great parts of the empire must not be misunderstood. They were an involuntary but necessary response to adverse conditions that had been developing since Valerian's departure.

"The political turbulence of the mid-third century frequently resulted in divided loyalties, but these were usually resolved relatively quickly. Either the contender was eliminated or he supplanted the established emperor. The phenomenon of a sustained division of loyalties, lasting for years on end, was unprecedented. In the aftermath of Valerian's disastrous defeat, as Gallienus struggled to reassert his authority in the central part of the empire, rivals inevitably filled the void elsewhere. The paramount need for an emperor on the spot prompted usurpations both in the east, where the Persian army was rampaging virtually unhindered, and in the west, where the Franks were constantly breaching the empire's defenses. At the same time, the Danube frontier remained constantly vulnerable to attack. These exceptionally serious external military threats allowed the political divisions to persist, effectively creating a *tripartite empire*. (...) Even though the empire had come close to political fragmentation, there was always a strong underlying cohesion in the empire as a whole. The world which Aurelian reunited through his victory at Châlons was, thus,

62

not an artificial construct held together by imperialist oppression. The great majority of Aurelian's subjects clearly shared his view that it was a world worth restoring.[194"]

Gaul and Palmyra allowed Rome to breathe again after decades of apnea. Without the efforts of these two political entities it is very likely that the empire would not have been able to recover itself. Although Roman prestige was seriously injured by the ambitions of these domains, the gain in material terms more than compensated for the loss of honour.

In fact, Aurelian implemented his reunification project only when he had settled the situation on the Danube, which was made possible by those who had divided the empire. After years of civil war and continuing instability, the Roman troops were no longer able to protect such a vast domain.

"The *vexillationes* (detachments from legions) and the auxiliary troops concentrated on the Rhine could be moved along the middle section of the Danube in a few weeks' time; considering a marching day of eight hours, at a speed of about four and a half kilometres per hour, the infantry (without loads) could take less than fifty days to march from the coast of the English Channel to the Black Sea. This meant that, during the summer and autumn months, when organized barbarian incursions were more frequent, it was possible that the same units would have to fight, in the same season, at opposite ends of the European borders of the empire.

The same thing could not happen, however, to the troops engaged in northern Mesopotamia, regardless of the success of their operations. Because of the greater distances, in fact, from the point of view of the system, the cost of war operations against Persia was disproportionate compared to the number of troops employed, however great this may have been. The dangers that threatened the Rhine and the Danube were endemic in nature, but only when another equally endemic danger appeared in the East did the overall burden on the shoulders of the forces at the disposal of the empire reveal itself in all its gravity.[195"]

---

[194] A. Watson, *Aurelian and the Third Century* (1999), Routledge, London, 2003, pp. 98-100.

[195] E. Luttwak, *The Grand Strategy of the Roman Empire* (1976), Bur Rizzoli, 2016, p. 280-281.

In light of the logistical and military difficulties of the empire, the choices of Gallienus and Aurelian certainly seem much more understandable. If the former had his hands somewhat tied, the latter took full advantage of the situation. Aurelian made use of the defensive cover offered by the Gallic Empire in the West and the Kingdom of Palmyra in the East, stabilizing his position in Italy before moving towards the Danube. The usurpations therefore should be thought of as damaging to the emperors, but *not* to the empire. All rulers, from Gaul to Palmyra, all the way to the Eternal City, had in mind a single Roman homeland, and acted as one body to preserve it. The acumen of Gallienus and Aurelian was to promote a territorial retrenchment policy at a time when honour and prestige played a very important role. Unlike many rulers from the not too distant past, the two emperors understood that in order to emerge from the quagmire in which Rome found itself, they would need a strong push. They had no qualms about bending down, even very low. It was an unusual attitude, historically speaking, that turned out to be effective in the end.

Bust, probably of Aurelian. (© Wikicommons / Giovanni Dall'Orto)

Tetrarchy

"...after whom the gods gave us Diocletian and Maximian to be our princes, joining to these great men Galerius and Constantius, the one of whom was born to wipe out the disgrace incurred by Valerian's capture, the other to bring again the province of Gaul under the laws of Rome. Four rulers, indeed, of the world were they, brave, wise, kindly, and wholly generous[196]"

The *impero tripartito* model probably inspired in Diocletian a new division of the empire. Rising to power in 284, the new emperor was a military man of Illyrian origin, who won himself the right to don purple after defeating Marcus Aurelius Carinus, son of the late emperor Carus, in battle[197]. The start of his reign was not at all unlike others before it; Rome had become accustomed to power changing hands this way by the third century. Over time, Diocletian revealed himself to be one of the most capable and enduring sovereigns that Rome had ever had. It is no coincidence that modern historiography marks the end of the Crisis of the Third Century with the beginning of his rule. One of Diocletian's first provisions was the establishment of a "tetrarchy" (from the Greek τετραρχία, literally "government of four persons"), which divided the Roman Empire. Usurpers aside, the simultaneous presence of several emperors was a practice that had several precedents in Roman history: Augustus is one example, having brought several family members to power and Marcus Aurelius and Lucius Verus, from the previous chapter, are others. The reasons behind the new division are easy to understand. More than anything else, what had undermined the safety and health of Rome had been political instability, caused by the unchecked ambition of various military commanders at the borders. As we saw under Gallienus and for a few years under Aurelian, the empire resisted external threats much better if its government was divided among more actors. Clearly, one individual would have struggled to bear the heavy burdens that an empire like Rome imposed towards the end of the third century.

---

[196] Historia Augusta, *Carus, Carinus and Numerian*, 18, 3-4.
[197] V.A. Sirago, "Diocleziano", *Nuove questioni di storia antica*, Milan, 1967, pp. 3-4.

"Since 285, Diocletian found himself facing a troublesome external situation: on the Rhine, they were attacking the Alemanni, near the Danube, the Quadi, while in Gaul and along the coasts facing the English Channel, there were other disturbances. There were rebellions of an agrarian nature led by bands bearing the Celtic name of *Bacaudae* (or *Bagaudae*, the form and etymology remain doubtful) and raids carried out by the Franks and Saxons as well as other revolts in Syria and Egypt.[198]"

Necessity compelled Diocletian, not quite a year after taking power, to grant Maximian, a military officer of humble origins, the title of *Caesar*, and then *Augustus* a few months later, making him his equal in terms of the empire's leadership[199]. He understood that the only option was to share power; the emperor could not afford to face all the forces that threatened the borders alone. The diarchy had an immediately positive effect, largely due to Maximian's total loyalty to his colleague. Their roles were well defined, even at the religious level. Diocletian was the mind of the empire and for this he was given the title of *Iovius*, while Maximian was proclaimed *Heraclius*, the strong arm that would put Diocletian's strategies into action[200]. In this first division of power, Maximian settled in Mediolanum and assumed the task of honouring the heavy commitments presented by the Rhine front. Diocletian made his capital Nicomedia in Bithynia, which was strategically important due to the city's proximity to the Straits and its equidistance from the Danube and the Mesopotamian front. The division of obligations produced the desired effects. Maximian could concentrate first on resolving the centrifugal thrust of the *Bagaudae*, peasant groups from Gaul who rebelled against the ever-increasing taxes imposed by Rome. Later, he sent several expeditions from Mogontiacum to Germany Magna to attack the Alemanni and Franks[201].

---

[198] G.A. Cecconi, *Da Diocleziano a Costantino: le nuove forme del potere*, p. 46.

[199] V.A. Sirago, "Diocleziano", *Nuove questioni di storia antica*, Milan, 1967, pp. 4-5.

[200] G.A. Cecconi, *Da Diocleziano a Costantino: le nuove forme del potere*, p. 47.

[201] V.A. Sirago, "Diocleziano", *Nuove questioni di storia antica*, Milan, 1967, pp. 5.

Diocletian first turned his attention to the Danube, where he pacified several tribes that were applying pressure to the borders then focused on the Sasanian Empire. The efforts that Maximian had made not long before allowed him to initiate negotiations with the historic enemy to the East, which produced fruitful peace for the Romans.

Sculpture depicting the tetrarchs, the four sovereigns of the empire.
(© Wikicommons / Nino Barbieri)

In 293, despite the desired outcome, Diocletian decided to increase the number of rulers of Rome and instituted the Tetrarchy. Galerius and Constantius Chlorus were named *Caesares*, the former tasked with supporting Diocletian in the East and the latter with supporting Maximian in the West[202]. Although official sources continued to speak of a formally unified empire (proof being that panegyrics of the time used the words *patrimonium indivisum* or *imperium singulare*[203]), the

---

[202] Ibidem, pp. 7-8.
[203] G.A. Cecconi, *Da Diocleziano a Costantino: le nuove forme del potere*, p. 47.

Roman dominion was divided, especially for military reasons, into four parts. Constantius Chlorus assumed command of Gaul and Britain, setting up his strategic base at Augusta Treverorum (today's Trier); Maximian ruled Italy, northern Africa and Hispania from Mediolanum; Galerius was charged with protecting all of the Danubian and Balkan provinces, choosing Thessalonica as his capital; finally, Diocletian, the real linchpin of the tetrarchy, remained in Nicomedia, in command of the rich eastern provinces. The Tetrarchy was solidified by a studied family policy: Diocletian and Maximian were brothers by marriage, and Galerius and Constantius Chlorus were their adopted children, designated to replace them in the event of death or abdication. In the case of either of these eventualities, Galerius and Constantius would have become *Augusti*, and in turn they would have had to appoint two new *Caesares*, and so on. The division between senatorial provinces and imperial provinces utilized by Octavian Augustus was passed over for a division into twelve areas, called "dioceses" (each emperor was assigned three of them). The four parts of the empire were provided with mints, so that all of the emperors could have a certain amount of economic independence, especially when it came to military costs. The new Roman army, dramatically changed after the Diocletian reforms (more on that topic is forthcoming), was divided into two "mobile" armies which were in turn divided between the four jurisdictions. The effects were positive given that four emperors, rather than one alone, provided for the defense of the empire (and all of them had marked expertise in war). Constantius Chlorus quashed the rebellion led by Carausius, a usurper who had proclaimed himself emperor, and during his reign he managed to solidify the Rhine front[204]. Maximian, given that European threats were kept at bay by Constantius, gathered all the forces at his disposal for an African campaign against the Berbers, who were a scourge upon the coastal cities of northwest Africa[205].

---

[204] V.A. Sirago, "Diocleziano", *Nuove questioni di storia antica*, Milan, 1967, pp. 7-8.
[205] Ibidem.

With the blessing of Diocletian, Galerius assumed command of military operations in the East, anticipating a new conflict with the Persians. Despite a frustrating initial defeat[206], Galerius demonstrated his great qualities as a general, defeating the army of the King Narseh on several occasions, and conquering the capital Ctesiphon[207].

This co-ordination of defensive and offensive operations would have been impossible if Diocletian had decided to remain in command alone. Thus, the Diarchy, followed by the Tetrarchy, guaranteed the survival of the empire and created the conditions for its recovery. Just as the patient who is healing slowly returns to normal, so too, did Rome gradually return to what had distinguished it since its beginning; conquests, to be precise. Let us be clear, the empire remained in a situation of crisis, and even under the four emperors a territorial disengagement similar to the Agri Decumates and Dacia was necessary. As previously mentioned, in fact, the city of Volubilis was abandoned as was part of Mauretania, hardly defensible due to the predations of the Mauri. Lastly, the Dodecaschoenus, a region in Egypt, was entrusted to the control of the *foederati* Nobates.

However, the tetrarchic system made possible a variety of military operations that, under a monarchy, would have been unthinkable. Maximian, thanks to the presence of Constantius, was able to leave northern Italy for Africa, where he led a difficult campaign lasting two years (297-299) against the Mauri and Baquates, populations that had been attacking the southern limes with impunity for several decades. Diocletian's greatest governmental success materialized in the East, with Galerius' great victory over the Sassanids. The campaign of the two tetrarchs, during which the closest family members of the great Persian King Narseh were captured, had a huge impact. The Peace of Nisibis (299) ensured that the empire had five satraps beyond the Tigris[208], which functioned as a territorial buffer slowing down Persian advances towards Syria. The Roman influence on the Kingdom of Armenia and the Kingdom of Caucasian Iberia was guaranteed, and

---

[206] Eutropius, *Breviarium ab Urbe condita*, 9, 24.
[207] Ibidem, 9, 25.
[208] Ammianus Marcellinus, *History*, 25, 7, 9.

70

trade between the two empires was established with the city of Nisibis designated as the exclusive site of commerce[209]. In terms of territorial and diplomatic advantages, the victory of Galerius was undoubtedly the crowning achievement for the Romans, who had been battling against a renewed Persian enemy. This victory was the result of the political-military division of force at that time. The Tetrarchy did not last long. Once the role of Diocletian (the real architect of this governing structure) was exhausted, the jealousies and ambitions that had characterized the third century reappeared. Rome fell into a long and bloody civil war, from which emerged the illegitimate son of Constantius Chlorus, known to history as Constantine the Great. This does not detract from the fact that the Tetrarchy greatly benefited Rome. Indeed, it can be affirmed without question that this system of government gave the empire several additional decades of life.

The Grand Strategy

Towards the end of his rule, Octavian Augustus left very precise instructions to his successors: the empire had to settle disputes in the North on the Rhine and Danube, and in the East on the Euphrates. The progressive ending of conquests led the Romans to formulate a grand strategy to defend their immense empire. The concept of a grand strategy was introduced to the study of Roman history for the first time through the literary contributions of Edward Luttwak, who sparked a debate that still persists today. Before outlining its merits, it is first useful to define the meaning of this concept:

"(The grand strategy is) the set of all the political, military and economic objectives, pursued both in peace and in war, aimed at preserving long-term interests, including the management of ends and means, of diplomacy, of national morale and political culture, both in the civil and military spheres.[210]"

---

[209] Festus, *Breviarium rerum gestarum populi Romani*, 14-25.
[210] P. Kennedy, *Grand Strategy in War and Peace: Toward a Broader Definiton*, in Kennedy, *Grand Strategies in War and Peace*, ix, 4-5.

Although Luttwak's work is bold and at times tends to use a "modern lens" when analysing the ancient world, critics of his like Benjamin Isaac[211] go too far, dismissing the idea that Rome may have made strategic choices.

"The Romans did not demarcate their eastern border and thought, in geographic terms, presumably in terms of peoples rather than territory, so there was no "line in the sand" marked by detachments of existing troops and forts. Further, neither deployments nor forts (in Isaac's view) offer any key to their actual use. Eastern legions tended to be based in cities rather than directly on a supposed frontier, and "border" forts, never impregnable tactical structures, merely protected lines of communication, housed soldiers assigned to internal security, or were not forts at all but road stations for travellers. In sum, Isaac can find no evidence of a centralized "grand strategy," a consistent strategy in any sense, or even defensive thinking. Geographical ignorance, absence of a general staff, and the lack of a professional officer class eliminate use of strategy in practice, as the omission of strategy in ancient military manuals does in theory. All depends on the whims of individual emperors.[212]"

Isaac's perspective[213] is reductionist and at times negligent, since he deliberately ignores those passages from ancient sources that contain considerable strategic references. Does it not seem that the Augustan desire to put certain limits on expansion[214] or the plan of Septimius Severus to make northern Mesopotamia an intended salient for the defense of Syria[215] were evidence of a grand strategy? Certainly, the Romans never adopted a purely defensive mentality, not even when their empire found itself in crisis; the expedition of Maximinus Thrax to the heart of Germania Magna (235) or the Sarmatian campaigns of Valentinian I (374 -375) are examples of this. Centuries-old traditions in Roman military leadership managed to overcome what many have

---

[211] Benjamin Isaac is an Israeli professor of ancient history who, with his work "The Limits of the Empire: The Roman Army in the East", took a critical stance on Luttwak's work.

[212] E.L. Wheeler, *Methodological Limits and the Mirage of Roman Strategy: Part I*, p. 11.

[213] B. Isaac, "The Meaning of the Terms Limes and Limitanei", *The Journal of Roman Studies*, Vol. 78 (1988), pp. 125-147.

[214] Tacitus, *Annals*, 1, 11 , 8 and *Agricola*, 13, 2.

[215] Cassius Dio, *Roman History*, 75, 3, 2-3.

defined as insurmountable disadvantages[216]. A certain strategic effort can be noted, for example, in the location of the legions on the imperial territory.

"(...) If the Romans understood all the subtleties of strategy, "they kept quiet about it," in other words no surviving articulations on strategy survive. Yet this is not quite true. Tacitus, for one, was able to talk explicitly in terms of mobile defense at a strategic level. In his well-known description of the army's dispositions in ad 14 (Ann. 4.5), he says: "But our main strength (*praecipuum robur*) was the eight legions on the Rhine, as a reserve (*subsidium*) against both the Germans and the Gauls." In the same passage, he speaks of the two legions stationed in Dalmatia as "backing up" the other four on the Danube, but also able to move swiftly to Italy if "assistance at short notice" (*auxilium repentinum*) was needed there. This is a strategy of mobile defense, if anything is.[217]"

The legionary and auxiliary troops were stationed regionally, near the *limites*, ready to face the enemy. In the early days of the Roman Empire, from Augustus to Nero, Luttwak argues that Rome continued the policy of "hegemonic expansionism" from the late Republican period, managing to establish a balance between a system of direct control and a system of indirect control. There were only 28 legions to protect the immense Roman Empire though they were supported by so-called client kingdoms; as such, potential external threats had to first confront Rome's allies, who repelled or at least slowed them down while awaiting the arrival of Roman legions[218]. The second model, called "advanced defense" (or preventive defense), was employed from the Flavians to the Severi, consisted in identifying, intercepting and annihilating threats *beyond* Roman borders. During this period, the Romans slowly assimilated all their client kingdoms to create a contiguous external frontier that they could defend. In doing so, Rome took on all the costs of defense for threats of varying size, from

---

[216] Just think of the quality of Roman generals: Drusus Major, Tiberius, Germanicus and Corbulo showed themselves capable countless times of conceiving of tactically and strategically valuable moves.

[217] P. Erdkamp, *A Companion to the Roman Army*, Blackwell Publishing, 2007, p. 229.

[218] E. Luttwak, *The Grand Strategy of the Roman Empire* (1976), Bur Rizzoli, 2016, p. 30-98.

encroaching marauders to large-scale barbarian invasions [219]. This system hit a crisis during the reign of Marcus Aurelius. The Marcomanni had shown themselves to be formidable invaders. Once they had broken through the border defenses, for weeks they were able to spread out into the imperial territory before being intercepted by the Roman legions. As we have already seen, the mobility of forces at the time was quite limited. Journey time from the capital to Colonia Agrippina (modern-day Cologne in Germany) was 67 days while it was as long as 124 days to Antioch[220].

The increasingly frequent attempts to penetrate the borders had already forced Septimius Severus to make some of the first changes to the Roman military-strategic apparatus. The first central strategic reserve[221] was established and stationed near Albanum (20 kilometres from the capital). Its task was to resolve possibly critical situations on imperial territory. This force, consisting predominantly of the *Legio II Parthica* (5,500 to 6,000 men), was flanked by 11,000 elite soldiers from praetorian cohorts and cavalrymen from the emperor's personal guard (the *Equites Singulares Augusti*), plus thousands of other urban cohorts and *vigiles*, for a total of about 30,000 armed men[222]. Severian reforms, due to the volatile and changeable climate of the empire, were adhered to only from the beginning of the second half of the third century. The first to understand that the Roman army needed to be completely reformed was once again Gallienus[223]. Because of the scarcity of men and intensifying assaults by the enemy, the empire could no longer rely entirely on the rigid defense presented by the *limites*. The imperial units had to be able to move with great speed in order to intercept the barbarian hordes that were flowing into Roman territory; for this

---

[219] E.L. Wheeler, "Methodological Limits and the Mirage of Roman Strategy: Part I", *The Journal of Military History*, Vol. 57, No. 1 (Jan., 1993), pp. 7-41.

[220] E. Luttwak, *The Grand Strategy of the Roman Empire* (1976), Bur Rizzoli, 2016, p. 156.

[221] R. E. Smith, "The Army Reforms of Septimius Severus", *Historia: Zeitschrift für Alte Geschichte*, Franz Steiner Verlag, Bd. 21, H. 3 (3rd Qtr., 1972), pp. 487-488.

[222] Ibidem.

[223] S. MacDowell, *Late Roman Infantryman 236-565 AD*, Reed Consumer Books, London, 1994, p. 3.

purpose, the heavy legionary infantry had become unsuitable, due to their very limited mobility[224]. Gallienus chose to leave most of the infantry to guard the borders, concentrating his efforts on developing troops on horseback. The imperial forces had already been equipped with specialized cavalry units under Trajan and Hadrian. As time passed, more and more emperors, from Septimius Severus to Maximinus Thrax, made extensive use of these units with excellent results[225]. However, it was only under the son of Valerian that a crucial change was made: separate cavalry units were created, independent of legions. Several coins issued under Gallienus in the two-year period between 259 and 260 indicate the names of legionary units that were still stationed within the territories controlled by the Gallic Empire or the Kingdom of Palmyra. The *denarii* likely referred to detachments (*vexillationes*) originally belonging to those legions that were then outsourced to form part of a completely new military cavalry. Fittingly, the coins bear the legend "FIDES EQUITUM"[226].

This mobile army was formed by the *equites promoti*, taken from the legionary and auxiliary units, and was augmented by the *equites Dalmatae et Mauri*, the *equites scutarii, stablesiani, sagittarii* and *armigeri*[227]. Gallienus located their bases in Mediolanum (northern Italy), Lychnidos (Macedonia), and Sirmium and Poetovio (Pannonia) in order to facilitate the action of the cavalry. The *equites* were thereby already near the borders. The Mediolanum base was an excellent starting point for blocking possible invasions by the Alemanni who, in occupying the Agri Decumates, had come very close to Italy, while the other three bases were better situated for fending off raiders from the many tribes living near the Danube[228]. Gallienus also increased the cavalry present in each legion from 120 units to 726 units, making the legions even more mobile[229]. However, the core of the "field" army was

---

[224] Ibidem.

[225] Historia Augusta, *The Two Maximini*, 11-12.

[226] L. de Blois, *The Policy of the Emperor Gallienus*, E.J. Brill, Leiden, 1997, pp. 26-30.

[227] Ibidem.

[228] Ibidem, pp.30-31.

[229] Ibidem, p.27

made up of units on horseback, which did not respond to any orders from the provincial governor, but only to those of the emperor and the *magister equitum*. This last figure, exemplifying the importance given to the new institutions established by Gallienus, became *de facto* the second most powerful person in the empire[230].

Although the use of units selected from legions and *auxilia* was a well-established practice among the emperors (consider the large number of *vexillationes* used by Trajan in the Dacian Wars or by Marcus Aurelius during the Marcomannic Wars), the strategic-military reforms of Gallienus were an *ad hoc* response that in fact proved decisive for the fate of the empire. The concept of strategic reserves created by Septimius Severus was developed and the groundwork was laid for reforms drawn up between the end of the third century and the beginning of the fourth century[231].

---

[230] Ibidem, p.26
[231] Ibidem, p.36

Bust of Gallienus, who initiated Rome's recovery.
(© Wikicommons/Capillon)

The function of bases with mobile units is also worth a closer look. As we have seen, these strongholds were located at strategically vital points, not in close proximity to the borders but rather, in the interior of the imperial territory[232]. This was due to the fact that fixed linear defense systems were by now unsustainable for the Roman economy. So military centres were set up in all the so-called "intermediate" regions (Cisalpine Gaul, Raetia, Pannonia, Noricum, Thrace, Syria) in order to be able to erect a protective shield within the most important, internal areas of the empire[233].

The key points of the new Roman defense were Cologne on the Rhine front, Siscia and Sirmium on the Danube, Byzantium on the Aegean, and Antioch and Samosata in Mesopotamia. In this context, the defense of northern Italy, the access route to the capital, was of tremendous importance. Mediolanum, Verona and Aquileia became fortresses with substantial garrisons; these strategic centres were entrusted to the *magister equitum* of Gallienus, Manius Acilius Aureolus, who was awarded the title of *dux per Raetias* for this responsibility[234]. This office had a precedent, during the reign of Marcus Aurelius. In the aftermath of the fall of the Macromanni, the philosopher emperor established a military district (the *Praetentura Italiae et Alpium*) which included part of north-eastern Italy, the Julian Alps, and vast areas of the provinces of Raetia and Noricum. As did Gallienus, Marcus Aurelius tasked a man of undoubted military qualities with the command of this area, who was awarded the prestigious title of *Augusti ad praetenturam Italiae et Alpium expeditione Germanica legatus*[235].

---

[232] Ibidem, pp. 30-34.

[233] Ibidem.

[234] Ibidem.

[235] The *legatus Augusti* was a man of senatorial rank who was honoured with the *imperium* (power of a military nature) directly by the emperor; it was, in short, a role that involved great responsibility.

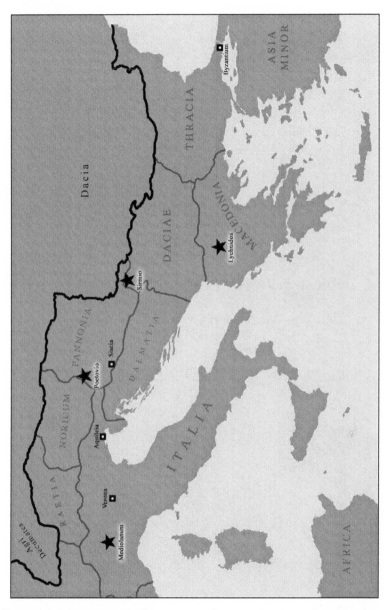

Gallienus' defense system in the interior: the stars represent the main bases of the cavalry units and the squares represent the fortified cities during this period. (© Davide Montingelli)

It is clear that the establishment of a fortified interior with mobile units was a particularly effective measure against intense threats such as those represented by Marcomanni and Alemanni. Even after the death of Gallienus, the Romans still preferred cavalry that could be considered an "elastic defense" in strategic terms. The border troops were almost always hit by large barbarian hordes who, having crossed into imperial territory could continue to penetrate for hundreds of kilometres, at which point the central Roman reserves, positioned near the *limites*, could intervene.

"In this case (that of *elastic defense*), in fact, the defense is based exclusively on the mobility of the troops, which should be at least equal to that of the enemy offensive. The two adversaries thus fight on equal terms: the defense can count on a concentration of forces equal to that of the enemies, not having to assign units as fixed-position garrisons or employing detachments of soldiers to protect the remaining territory; on the other hand, the defense is forced in this way to sacrifice all the tactical advantages normally associated with its role (except knowledge of the terrain), since neither of the two adversaries can choose the place of the fight nor prepare it by building undisturbed fortification works.[236]"

This strategy could work as an *extrema ratio* and enemies could eventually be defeated... but at what price? In 258, the Franks crossed the Iberian Peninsula, even reaching Gibraltar, while Gallienus stopped a Marcomanni raid near Ravenna[237]. Aurelian also had to face a major invasion on the Italian peninsula, this time from the Juthungi. These barbarians used Roman roads but were difficult to locate for imperial troops at first. In the end, however, they were intercepted and defeated first at Fanum[238] and then at Ticinum, in 271.

The problem with this strategy was that the time between the first threat from the encroaching barbaric hordes and their interception by Roman mobile troops was too long; the damages suffered were oftentimes devastating.

---

[236] E. Luttwak, *The Grand Strategy of the Roman Empire* (1976), Bur Rizzoli, 2016, p. 245.

[237] Eutropius, *Breviarium ab Urbe condita*, 9, 7.

[238] Historia Augusta, *Aurelian*, 18-19.

The empire's political situation, which was plagued by instability after Gallienus and Aurelian, prevented Roman rulers from making significant strategic changes, at least until the Tetrarchy.

Defense-in-depth

"For the Roman Empire, as I have related, was, by the care of Diocletian, divided (...) into towns, fortresses and towers. Since the army was positioned everywhere, the barbarians could not penetrate it. Troops were ready to oppose invaders and prevent them from making inroads.[239]"

In only a few lines, the Greek historian Zosimus testifies to what Luttwak calls "defense-in-depth[240]"; that is, the new defense system adopted by the Roman Empire towards the end of the third century. After bringing three other generals like him to the throne, Diocletian began to overhaul the Roman war machine, which had long been in need of change. The imperial army, which was mainly divided into two types of units, was radically altered.

"To create an effective mobile army, Diocletian reorganized the Roman army and divided it into two parts, *comitatenses* and *limitanei*. (...) The *comitatenses* were mobile, land groups that were settled in the hinterland of the Empire. They were placed in strategically suitable points, always near important roads, which allowed easy movement from one part of the state to the other. In this way it was possible to guarantee help whenever it was necessary. The soldiers (the *comitati*) were young and had no family. The other group, the *limitanei*, was formed as a border unit. These troops were stationary and represented a kind of peasant border police (...). The system of the limes had now changed and became a system reasonably equipped with fortifications and camps. The limes became in fact the border road, for the defense of which a complex system of ditches, trenches and fortresses was built.[241]"

---

[239] Zosimus, *New History*, 2, 34, 1.

[240] E. Luttwak, *The Grand Strategy of the Roman Empire* (1976), Bur Rizzoli, 2016, p. 245-356.

[241] E. Stankovic, *Diocletian's Military Reforms*, Acta Univ. Sapientiae, Legal Studies, 1, 1 (2012), p.133.

The army was extensively reorganized and the legions were reduced. Traditionally, a legionary unit had consisted of 5,500 to 6,000 soldiers; however, during the Tetrarchy it counted around 1,000 soldiers). This reduction increased their mobility[242]. Along with military reforms, an elaborate plan for defensive buildings was initiated. After mitigating Roman borders, the previous system of *limites* was abandoned in favour of a much wider defensive area, made up of different "fortress-cities".

Even before the Tetrarchy, Rome was fortified. Aurelian had equipped the capital with thick walls, which would have served as a "force multiplier" in the event of a large-scale invasion[243]. The objective of the new strategy was to let the invaders enter the empire knowing that the *limitanei* and complex system of fortifications would slow them down. Enemies, usually barbarians with little knowledge of how to lay siege, would have had to choose whether to try to take these forts or instead, venture deep into Roman territory, without much chance of finding loot or supplies. In fact, they would have been cut off from any supplies (since all the food supplies would have previously been located within the Roman fortifications). At this point the *limitanei* would have to wait for the *comitatenses*, the "real" army, which would have intercepted and neutralized the invaders[244].

---

[242] E. C. Nischer, "The Army Reforms of Diocletian and Constantine and Their Modifications up to the Time of the Notitia Dignitatum", *The Journal of Roman Studies*, Society for the Promotion of Roman Studies, Vol. 13 (1923), pp. 1-55.

[243] E. Luttwak, *The Grand Strategy of the Roman Empire* (1976), Bur Rizzoli, 2016, p. 91. Term from modern military lexicon that the author uses for Theodosian Walls.

[244] A. Ferrill, "Roman Imperial Grand Strategy", *Publication of the Association of Ancient Historians 3*, University Press of America, 1991, p.49.

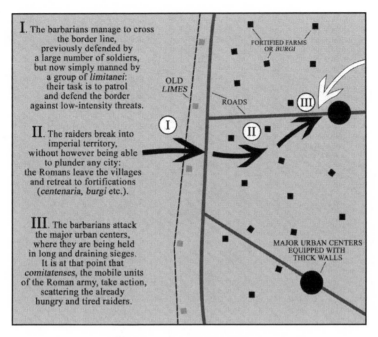

An example of defense-in-depth.

(© Davide Montingelli)

It was a socially expensive system since much of the security of the provincial centres was sacrificed yet it was generally advantageous, given that the number of soldiers needed to defend the borders was significantly lower than it had been before the Tetrarchy[245]. It is thanks to ancient sources we can identify two striking examples of this strategy from this period, which Luttwak calls "defense-in-depth": The Gothic campaign of Claudius II (268-269) and the Gaul campaign of Julian (355-360).

In the first example, a massive horde of Goths arrived by sea from modern-day Ukraine. The barbarians attacked coastal cities such as Marcianopolis and Byzantium. Their attempts to lay siege were, however, ineffective and the Goths were forced to withdraw to the sea.

---

[245] E. Luttwak, *The Grand Strategy of the Roman Empire* (1976), Bur Rizzoli, 2016, p. 353-356.

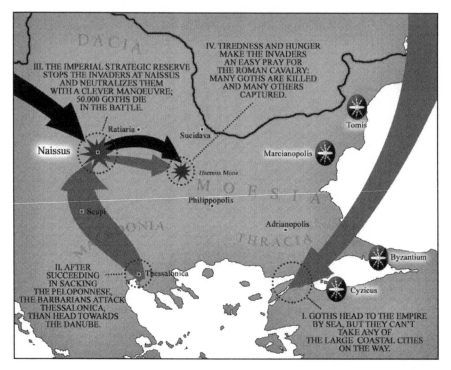

The development of Claudius II's Gothic campaign: after being unable to penetrate the fortified centres, the invaders were intercepted and neutralized by Rome's mobile forces.

(© Davide Montingelli)

Once they reached the Aegean Sea, the Goths managed to sack the inhabited centres that had not been fortified and then landed in Thessalonica. From there they headed northwards by land, going back over the limes with their loot.

During the journey they were intercepted by the Emperor Claudius II's strategic reserves; the Roman troops, commanded by Aurelian, massacred the Goths[246]. It was an impactful victory for the whole region; in fact, the barbarian tribe stopped antagonizing the Roman military authorities for several decades.

---

[246] Zosimus, *New History*, 1, 43.

The second case of "defense-in-depth" can be credited to the work of Ammianus Marcellinus. In the "Histories" of this historian of Late Antiquity it is written that, in reaction to the Alemanni's vast plundering, the emperor's first move was to liberate Augustodonum (today's Autun), which was under siege by the invaders[247]. This city was founded during the time of Augustus and was equipped with impenetrable walls at the beginning of the third century, as Ammianus Marcellinus mentions[248]. The Alemanni continued their aggressive campaign by attacking Lugdunum en masse but were thwarted by its dense walls and the efforts of the *limitanei*. The imperial *comitatus*, composed of 15,000 men, eventually clashed with the Alemannic horde of 35,000 men, near Argentoratum (present-day Strasbourg). Roman forces were unequivocally victorious and the barbarians retreated beyond the Rhine[249].

The respective victories of Claudius II and Julian are useful in understanding two aspects of "defense-in-depth," as it is called. The first is that, even in Late Antiquity, a Roman army in open battle could prevail over a more sizeable force. The military superiority of the imperial troops was not only the mark of forces during the second century but also of later forces, such as the comitatenses of the third and fourth centuries. The second is that, after the great victory obtained at Strasbourg, Julian crossed the Rhine and penetrated deep into the territory of the Alemanni, where he restored a fort from the Trajan era.

"Retaliatory action" was a practice that the Roman emperors had used since the early days of the empire (one example was the military campaign in Germany following the Teutoburg slaughter[250]). Legions plunged into enemy territory to punish those who had dared to attack Rome, or its allies. Despite military innovations, old habits continued to persist in uncertain times[251].

---

[247] Ammianus Marcellinus, *Histories*, 16, 1-11.
[248] Ibidem.
[249] Ibidem, 16, 12.
[250] Tacitus, *Annals*, 2, 22.
[251] M. Rocco, *Persistenze e cesure nell'esercito romano dai Severi a Teodosio I: ricerche in am-*

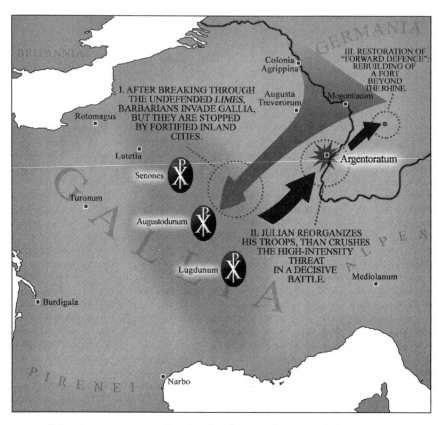

Julian's campaign in Gaul: after having devastated the interior,
the Romans engaged the Alemanni in small clashes.
The emperor only confronted them in open battle after reorganizing his troops
in the best possible way.

(© *Davide Montingelli*)

bito socio-politico, istituzionale, strategico, University of Padua, pp. 50-52.

The emperors did not in fact implement any systematic changes to their military strategy; instead, they responded in an *ad hoc* manner to situations that presented themselves from time to time.

Luttwak's work offers yet another astute observation on Roman defense-in-depth. The series of forts did not only extend inside, but also *outside* the Roman territory. Constantine had created extensive defenses beyond the Danube limes before Julian had begun to make his own sporadic efforts, as we have already mentioned.

The "Devil's Dam" in modern-day Hungary and the "Brazda lui Novac" ("Novac's Furrow" in Romanian) in Romania, were representative of these defenses, which consisted of about 700 km of fortifications protecting the Tisza River valley whose inhabitants were the Iazigi (at that time Roman allies). The border had several *burgi*, fortified villages, which were similar to the *centenaria* present in Tripolitania. Examples of these fortified outposts include Hatvan-Gombospuszta and Partiscum. These examples do not completely undermine the "defense-in-depth" thesis but rather, demonstrate that these defenses were not unusual.

"While on one hand, certain regions were abandoned given that they were not under direct military control, on the other, their sturdy forts acted as bridgeheads across the border, which made numerous offensive campaigns against neighbouring peoples possible, for the first time in almost a century.[252]"

The Roman defensive belt was much thicker than "The Grand Strategy of the Roman Empire" would have us believe; therefore, its depth, both inside and outside the empire, must be viewed with ambivalence.

---

[252] M. Rocco, *Persistenze e cesure nell'esercito romano dai Severi a Teodosio I: ricerche in ambito socio-politico, istituzionale, strategico*, University of Padua, pp. 213.

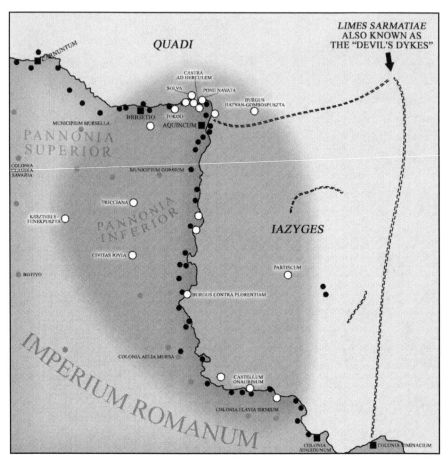

The Danube front from Pannonia: the white points are the defensive structures
built in Late Antiquity, the black points are the defensive structures built before,
the squares are the legionary fortresses and the grey points
represent inhabited centres.
The darker area represents the "depth" of the Roman defensive system,
seen both inside and outside the imperial borders.

(©Davide Montingelli)

Fortifications

As we have already explored, the new imperial strategy prominently featured fortified posts. The tetrarchs enlarged the existing forts, adding thicker walls and towers intended for the use of siege weapons. The fort of Sucidava, on the eastern bank of the Danube, had walls that went from being 1.6 metres think to 3 or even 4 metres thick by the beginning of the fourth century. Judging from archaeological excavations, new types of fortifications were eventually built, profoundly different from those of the empire in its early days, which were mainly in the formation of *castra*. A good model of military construction from the Diocletian Age is exemplified by the fort at Mobene[253] (Qasr Bshir), in the desert of Jordan. Located inside the *limes arabicus*, it was one of the strongholds used by the Romans to repel raids by desert tribes. The fort had a square shape (57 metres x 54 metres), with walls 1.5 metres thick and 6 metres high. Completing the structure were four imposing square towers about 12 metres high and projecting 3 metres from the walls[254]. On the European fronts smaller structures were widespread. The *quadriburgium* (there was one in Sapaja for example, which formed part of the Djerdap *limes*, in modern-day Serbia) had a square portico and four towers rising out of the corners as well as a *burgus*, was widely used both on the Rhine and Danube.

---

[253] "Mobene (Qasr Bshir)", *livius.org*, (retrieved February 17, 2018).
[254] Ibidem.

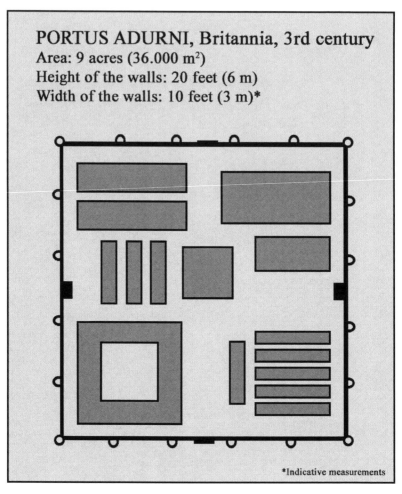

PORTUS ADURNI, Britannia, 3rd century
Area: 9 acres (36.000 m²)
Height of the walls: 20 feet (6 m)
Width of the walls: 10 feet (3 m)*

*Indicative measurements

Plan of the Roman fort of Portus Adurni, square in shape and built entirely in
stone. It was part of the defensive complex "Litus Saxonicum",
meant to protect against Saxon piracy.
The structure is an excellent example of the transformation that the imperial
castra underwent since the time of the first emperors
(rectangular and made of wood).

(© Davide Montingelli)

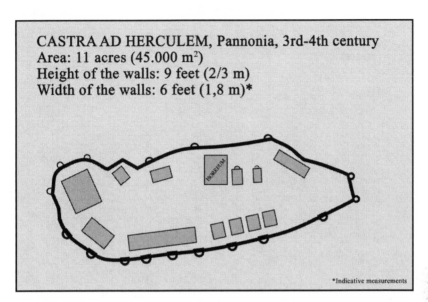

CASTRA AD HERCULEM, Pannonia, 3rd-4th century
Area: 11 acres (45.000 m²)
Height of the walls: 9 feet (2/3 m)
Width of the walls: 6 feet (1,8 m)*

*Indicative measurements

Plan of the fort of Castra ad Herculem. It was a defensive structure placed on a hill (the reason for its irregular plan), not far from the Danube river. The fort had a "horreum", a warehouse containing provisions for the Roman military.

(© Davide Montingelli)

This last type of fort had a square shape (with sides just under 20 metres) and a single internal tower supported by four large pillars. Such structures could contain a small garrison of *limitanei* and a discreet stock of supplies, however their purpose was probably only to signal to the enemy that the Roman forces were prepared and organized in their defensive operations[255]. In short, the new strategy was also reflected in the brickwork.

"The forts of late ancient Rome were usually built more robustly than their predecessors, with thicker walls bristling with towers. (...) The changes to the existing

---

[255] "Roman Limes: Frontier Line of the Roman Empire in the Iron Gate Area", *danube-cooperation.org*, (retrieved February 17, 2018).

forts radically changed their appearance. The Eining fort on the Danube is perhaps the most famous example of a very small fort. This late ancient fortress is squashed into the corner of the former fort, separated from it by its own moat. (...) At *Ulcisia Castra*, renamed *Castra Constantia*, located south of the Danube, all the gates except one were blocked by the addition of protruding towers in the shape of 'D'. These were added to the already existing square towers that flanked the entrance. The walls were reinforced with the addition of projecting interspersed towers and all four corners received the distinctive fan-shaped towers that protruded both internally and externally.[256]"

As reported in the opening passage by the historian Zosimus, the border areas were covered by a dense network of fortifications and fortresses. This system worked only *if* the defensive complex had the minimum garrison available to be manned. However, across the empire during the fourth century this practice was often disregarded. Julian was forced to move his *comitatus* in Gaul because a usurper named Magnentius had emptied the region of all his troops to fight against the emperor in the East, Constantius II[257]. This situation had facilitated the actions of the Alemanni, who crossed the Rhine and devastated many Roman cities. Julian intervened, but what was the price paid by the local civil population? The Gallic countryside was devastated, large centres such as Colonia Agrippina, Mogontiacum and Borbetomagus were looted and about 20,000 inhabitants were enslaved [258]. The problem with defense-in-depth was precisely this: it gave priority to the security of the whole empire but to the detriment of particular parts of it. Therefore, if, on one hand it can be said that the new system was effective then on the other, it can certainly be said that it played a role nurturing popular dissatisfaction towards the imperial government[259].

---

[256] K.R. Dixon, P. Southern, *Late Roman Army*, 1996, p.133.

[257] Zosimus, *New Story*, 2, 42, 2-5.

[258] Emperor Julian, *Letter to the Athenians*, 280.

[259] E. Luttwak, *The Grand Strategy of the Roman Empire* (1976), Bur Rizzoli, 2016, p. 356.

The role of allies in Rome's Grand Strategy

During the reign of Augustus, the Roman Empire had made alliances with several states, especially in the East. These kingdoms, modest from the point of view of a major military power, played a role of considerable strategic importance, nonetheless. First of all, they halted all low-intensity threats (marauders, bandits, etc.) thus creating an effective barrier to the empire. They were also useful as diplomatic "buffers" for major threats (such as the Parthians on the eastern front). Finally, they almost entirely assumed the costs of border defense; in fact, the legions intervened only in the case of large-scale invasions. Although over the decades the Romans annexed many of these client kingdoms, these alliances allowed Rome to project a powerful image. Rome succeeded in indirectly transmitting its power beyond its conventional boundaries at a considerably lower cost than a real military campaign would have required.

"It is, however, quite clear that by establishing and maintaining intensive contacts into the *barbaricum* the Roman emperors of the Principate had a profound influence on the political landscape immediately beyond the provincial frontiers. Indeed, it is possible to say that much of the barbarian world of *gentes* was to a great extent the result of Roman policy: *The Germanic world was perhaps the greatest and most enduring creation of Roman political and military genius.* Gaining control over this "Germanic world" was more important to the emperor than the creation of new provinces, as it significantly increased the security of a broad cordon of land separating the empire from the *barbaricum*. Within this cordon the construction of fortified provincial borders (e.g. the *limes* in Germany) was only one, albeit important, measure to mark the course of the frontier and at the same time to control the exchange of people and goods.[260]"

---

[260] P. Erdkamp, *A Companion to the Roman Army*, Blackwell Publishing, 2007, p.497.

Eastern client kingdoms at the time of the Julio-Claudians.

(© Davide Montingelli)

The strategy of "divide and rule" worked for centuries, allowing Rome to operate with great authority in territories that in fact did not belong to it. Starting from the Crisis of the Third Century, contact with the barbarian populations increased and relationships with them became even more complex. Finding themselves in a difficult military and demographic position, the Romans made extensive use of one diplomatic tool: money. In some cases, the emperors sought to render the tribes beyond the Rhine and Danube obedient with lavish subsidies; in other cases, they sought to co-opt entire populations into their ranks.

From the Severi onwards, the empire recorded innumerable internal struggles and plagues, which devastated many Roman units. Sometimes generals along the borders turned into usurpers. They convinced men from defeated tribes to support their personal claims for the throne in exchange for generous rewards and loot. It would have been too time-consuming to train new imperial troops and for that reason they began to recruit soldiers from the populations that were beyond the Roman borders.

So began what historians call the "barbarization" of the Roman army. Marcus Aurelius and his son Commodus had already used a modest number of barbarians but it was under the Severi that it became a practice. The archaeological evidence tells us that more and more *gentiles* (barbarians defeated in battle by the Romans) were employed by the imperial armies in the campaigns against the Sassanids. Caracalla, for example, co-opted several soldiers of Germanic and Danubian ethnicity for his expedition against Artabanus V, while Alexander Severus and Maximinus Thrax effectively used horsemen from the East in their expeditions to Magna Germania[261]. All these units remained "unofficial" at least until the rise of Diocletian. During the Tetrarchy, foreign departments became a regular and integral part of the comitatenses. There was a mounted unit of Marcomanni called *vexillatio equitum Marcomannorum*, which was brought by the emperor Probus to Egypt in 279 and remained there until at least 286[262]. In more than one case these forces became potent offensive posts for the Roman army and acquired the status of elite forces over time. The Cornuti, Brachiati and Petulanti were members of tribes from present-day Denmark that were organized by Constantine the Great in what was known as the *auxilia palatina*. We know that they fought fiercely in the Battle of the Milvian Bridge in 312[263].

---

[261] Historia Augusta, *The Two Maximini*, 11-12.
[262] P. Erdkamp, *A Companion to the Roman Army*, Blackwell Publishing, 2007, p.279.
[263] Ibidem.

The barbarians also constituted a discreet defensive force.

"With a large number of barbarians nonetheless serving in the Roman army, it was therefore crucial for the future of the empire in general and the Roman army in particular whether these "gentile Verbände" beyond Rhine and Danube could be successfully integrated into the military structures of the empire, or not. The first region of interest in this context is northern Gaul; because of its proximity to the Rhine frontier it allows valuable insight into how the defensive structures worked in Late Antiquity. From the third century onwards, it is possible to observe how the imperial government and the provincial administrations by a host of different measures reorganized the defense of the provinces; in these schemes, settlers and soldiers of barbarian origin assumed an increasingly important role. Thus from 297 onwards the so-called *laeti* (Pan. Lat. 8[5].21.1) are attested in the surviving sources; these were farmers of mainly Germanic origin who after their defeat had been allowed to settle in homogeneous settlements (*terrae laeticae*), which were under the control of the military administration. In times of war these *laeti* served under *praefecti laetorum*, officers appointed specifically for that task. Already in 232, the so-called *gentiles* are mentioned (CIL 13.6592 = Dessau, ILS 9184), who apparently were barbarian settlers as well, and they too, albeit not as often as the *laeti*, are mentioned as serving in the Roman army. It is still not totally clear how these *gentiles* differed from the *laeti* as far as their origin, legal status, and military deployment are concerned.[264]"

The Romans succeeded, through diplomacy (abetted by certain amounts of gold), in attracting many former enemies of the empire beneath their banners. The integration carried out by the Illyrian emperors up to and including Diocletian was a demonstrably effective policy that guaranteed troops who specialized in defending the empire for several decades. However, this process led to increasing external pressure on the Roman *res militaris*, which caused its substantial change. Even as early as the reign of Constantine, it was clear that tactics, equipment and military organization had profoundly changed compared to those used a century before by Septimius Severus. Although these changes did not significantly reduce the effectiveness of the Roman army, they did tip the balance and put the imperial war machine in a precarious position, which was increasingly moving towards these *novi milites*.

---

[264] Ibidem, pp. 499-500.

This delicate situation reached its dramatic conclusion in 378, in Adrianopole[265].

Military reorganization

The institution of the Roman military persisted almost unchanged for a long time and enjoyed numerous successes throughout the first part of the empire. Popular culture is familiar with the Roman army of that period, which was the fruit of Augustan military reforms. These were put in place shortly after Rome emerged from decades of civil war, which had militarized and drained the Italian peninsula. Octavian had to therefore utilize an intelligent economic-military relief policy. One of the first provisions of the *princeps* was to reduce the disproportionate number of armies used in recent infighting. In the Battle of Philippi in 42 B.C., there were about 250,000 soldiers on the field, which included the forces of the Second Triumvirate and the "Liberators". Just one year before Octavian's assumption of power in Actium, 35 legions and nearly 800 warships fought among themselves[266]. Augustus dissolved countless legions and provided for the retirement of many veterans, as he himself states.

"The Roman citizens who took the soldier's oath of obedience to me numbered about 500,000. I settled rather more than 300,000 of these in colonies or sent them back to their hometowns after their period of service; to all these I assigned lands or gave money as rewards for their military service.[267]"

---

[265] The Battle of Adrianople (378) was one of the greatest defeats in Roman imperial history. The Eastern Roman Emperor Valens also lost his life. From this moment onwards, the empire, especially in the West, had no choice but to tolerate large migratory waves over its borders.

[266] P. Erdkamp, *A Companion to the Roman Army*, Blackwell Publishing, 2007, pp. 184-185 and A. Ferrill, "Roman Imperial Grand Strategy", *Publication of the Association of Ancient Historians 3*, University Press of America, 1991, pp. 1-2.

[267] O. Augustus, *Res Gestae Divi Augusti*, 3.

In the end, he kept 28 legions active (25 after the *Clades Variana*[268]), which was a very small number of men considering that in the ancient world human strength was equivalent to military strength and that by this time, the empire was now an immense domain with many borders to protect. Nevertheless, legion numbers only ever changed in response to a handful of particular situations; they remained more or less unchanged for 250 years. When Tiberius became emperor, the legionary troops counted 125,000 men. These were augmented by 125,000 auxiliaries, 10,000 variously armed individuals in the capital and 40,000 sailors in the Misenum and Ravenna fleets, for a total of 300,000 [269]. Trajan increased the number of legions to 30 in line with his expansionist policy; with 165,000 legionaries[270] and about 220,000 auxiliaries, the army counted about 380,000 men (not including the sailors and naval personnel on the fleets). The Roman army was founded not on quantity, but on quality. Augustus made the Roman army a professional collective, consisting mainly of two components: the first was made up of Roman citizens (legionaries) who committed themselves to 20 years; the second was made up of non-Roman citizens (auxiliaries) who committed themselves for a longer period of 25 years[271].

---

[268] Another name for the defeat at the Battle of Teutoburg Forest, in which three legions were annihilated by the traitor Arminius.

[269] Y. Le Bohec, *The Imperial Roman Army*, Rome 2008, pp. 34-36.

[270] The number of men in the first cohort was doubled between Augustus and the Flavians.

[271] R. Cowan, *Roman Legionary 58 BC - 69 AD*, Osprey Publishing, 2003, pp. 12-13.

	TIBERIUS	TRAJAN	DIOCLETIAN
LEGIONARY FORCES (LEGIONS NUMBER)	125.000 (25)	165.000 (30)	390.000 (39 → 59)
AUXILIARY FORCES	125.000	220.000	
NAVAL FORCES AND SPECIAL UNITS	50.000	65.000	45.000
TOTAL	300.000	450.000	430.000

Roman army size during the imperial age. (© Davide Montingelli)

The legions consisted of 5,000 soldiers who were accompanied by 120 units on horseback. The cavalry in the legions did not play a particularly important role. Despite the appreciation among the Roman military for Alexander the Great and his impressive victories attained through the command of squadrons of *etairoi*[272], resistance to troops on horseback persisted for decades. For this reason, the Romans always relied on provincial troops to compensate. The legion infantry was divided into 10 cohorts each consisting of 480 men; each cohort was in turn formed by 6 centuries. Although many see the cohort as the tactical unit *par excellence* of the Roman army during this period, it could not have been since it lacked its own commander.

The century, commanded by the vital figure of the centurion, was certainly better suited to fill this role[273]. It was a unit that had stable and lasting command; this was not a feature of the legion as a whole because its commander, the *legatus legionis*, held his post for only about 3 years.

---

[272] These were a select group chosen from Alexander's army who were closest to the Macedonian ruler.

[273] R. Cowan, *Roman Legionary 58 BC - 69 AD*, Osprey Publishing, 2003, pp. 8-9.

Within the legion, the first cohort deserves attention. It was made up of 5 centuries instead of 6 but with twice as many men (160 instead of 80)[274]. The unit was commanded by the *primus pilus*, who was an experienced individual and whose rank was the only one equal to the rank of officer according to the modern meaning of the term. This special role, which also required him to protect the *aquila*, the legion's standard, could only be assumed after no less than 15 years of service[275].

The auxiliary troops, as explained in the preceding paragraphs, were composed of inhabitants from the provinces not yet in possession of Roman citizenship. The role that they played in the army was of equal importance compared to that of the legions. The Roman army's heavy infantry became famous throughout the world for being superbly efficient, but it was in large part thanks to the *auxilia* acting as support units for the legions[276]. These ethnically diverse troops could only be grouped into cohorts of infantry, similar in number to those of the legions but almost always composed of archers or slingers. Then there were the *alae*, units typically composed of 500 units on horseback with tasks ranging from simple reconnaissance to fighting on the front lines in battle, as well as the mixed cohorts, composed of troops on foot and on horseback[277]. Although the efforts of the provincial troops were of great help in defending the borders, the "central core" of the army remained the legion.

From the reign of Augustus onwards, every heavy infantryman in the Roman army was similarly equipped and considered, above all else, a swordsman. The legionary's main weapon was the *gladius hispaniensis*[278] (so named for the swords used by the people of the Iberian Peninsula). It was a double-edged sword of medium length (it was on average

---

[274] Ibidem, pp. 7-8.

[275] Ibidem.

[276] A. Goldsworthy, *The Complete Roman Army*, Thames and Hudson, 2003, pp. 55-58.

[277] Ibidem.

[278] R. Cowan, *Roman Legionary 58 BC - 69 AD*, Osprey Publishing, 2003, pp. 28-30. However, during the time of Octavian, the Mainz/Fulham sword and the Pompeii style sword were already being put to use, and both of them were better designed than their predecessor from the Republican era.

between 64 and 69 centimetres long and between 4 and 5.5 centimetres wide) and was very effective in inflicting injuries. The *pilum* shared the same notoriety as the *gladius*. This was a sharp, short-range throwing weapon ideal for punching through shields, armour and, of course, human beings. Approximately 2 metres long, this javelin was equipped with a metal tip as long as 90 centimetres and was often used in the early stages of battle prior to the *gladii*. Before the opposing sides crossed swords, the legionaries launched a volley of *pila*, doing considerable damage to the other side; at this point, the Romans would charge and devastate the enemy[279]. The imperial troops could also count on a more compact bladed weapon, the *pugio*, which was a dagger about 20 to 35 centimetres long[280]. Most emblematic of the equipment was the breastplate. The *lorica segmentata* was the most popular, judging by the Trajan Column. Interestingly, archaeological evidence found on the Kalkriese site, where the Battle of Teutoburg Forest took place, indicates that it had already been in use under Augustus[281]. Its form offered generous coverage of the torso and shoulders protecting the body from sword slashes and arrows. However, its leather components and hinges made of bronze and orichalcum made its maintenance both difficult and expensive[282]. The other breastplate used by the Roman troops was the *lorica hamata*, which was made of mesh and metal rings, and weighed up to 16 kilograms (as opposed to the *lorica segmentata's* 9 kilograms)[283]. Then there was the *scutum*, a rectangular curved shield that was initially light enough to be held with one hand (but later reinforced with metal plates) and could cover the entire body of the person holding it[284]. Its particular shape made tight formations possible, such as the famous *testudo*, which resembled a tortoise.

---

[279] Ibidem, pp. 25-26.

[280] Ibidem, p. 30.

[281] A. Goldsworthy, *The Complete Roman Army*, Thames and Hudson, 2003, pp. 126-129.

[282] Ibidem.

[283] R. Cowan, *Roman Legionary 58 BC - 69 AD*, Osprey Publishing, 2003, pp. 31-32.

[284] A. Goldsworthy, *The Complete Roman Army*, Thames and Hudson, 2003, pp. 129-130.

As for head gear, the Roman legionaries had already begun to abandon the helmets emblematic of the Republic under Julius Caesar, such as the Montefortino, in favour of Gallic and Italic types, which better protected the sides of the face[285]. The last element of the legion's equipment, although not the least important, was the spade.

"The Roman army on the march, when there was no immediate high intensity threat, dug a trench nine feet wide and seven feet deep around the encampment. If there was danger of immediate attack, the trench was twelve feet wide and nine feet deep. The excavated earth was thrown up around the trench and made it even deeper. Permanent camps had even wider trenches. Remains of Caesar's camps at Gergovia reveal some that were fifteen feet deep, and at Alesia there was a moat twenty feet wide. When Crassus cornered Spartacus in the toe of the Italian boot, he dug a trench thirty-four miles long, fifteen feet wide, and fifteen feet deep (...). It would not be an exaggeration to say that the spade was one of the most important weapons used by the Roman army. Its value was felt at all levels of warfare, tactics, operations and strategy. Because of the protection afforded by the Romans by their trenches and the capacity to hem an enemy in with the use of the spade, the Roman army was able to make barriers that would otherwise have required a much larger use of manpower. This skill is one of the many that relieved the strain on conscription.[286]"

This instrument revealed the great flexibility of the legionary troops, who were capable of constructing a bridge one moment and then annihilating a hostile force the next. The combination of engineering skills and discipline were the result of months of hard training. Recruits could expect long and exhausting marches in full armour, abiding by all the meticulous rules of the Roman army[287]. Once recruits became full-fledged soldiers, they still endured three regular marches each month, at the end of which they had to build a military camp complete with a moat and defensive palisade. The hard training and the strength built from wearing heavy equipment made the legions a devastating and unstoppable weapon against the enemies of Rome.

---

[285] R. Cowan, *Roman Legionary 58 BC - 69 AD*, Osprey Publishing, 2003, pp. 41-43.

[286] A. Ferrill, "Roman Imperial Grand Strategy", *Publication of the Association of Ancient Historians 3*, University Press of America, 1991, pp. 10-11.

[287] R. Cowan, *Roman Legionary 58 BC - 69 AD*, Osprey Publishing, 2003, pp. 11-12.

At some point, however, due to the causes that have already been extensively discussed, the efficient imperial war machine broke down. The next section details the reforms enacted between the end of the third century and the beginning of the fourth that Roman political actors used to attempt to respond to the great demands created by military changes.

Changes in demographics

Before arguing this point, it would be useful to dispel the bad reputation that many ancient and modern historians have attributed to Roman troops of Late Antiquity; that is, one of "crude barbarian peasants defending the empire" which does not correspond to the reality[288]. The Roman war machine, at least until the end of the fourth century, was as effective in its defensive tasks as the Principate troops were in their campaigns of conquest[289]. Indeed, it should be mentioned that the army of the late Roman Empire grew out of the old military system's failure to respond to the new needs of the empire. Any type of judgment or comparison should thus be avoided since the two armies took shape during different stages of the empire and had very different purposes.

"The recruitment of barbarians seems to have been fairly routine, and in principle was nothing new, for the *auxilia* of the Principate had also included men from outside the directly governed provinces. Yet we have no reliable statistics to establish the scale of barbarian recruitment in Late Antiquity. In the past it has often been seen as a sign of a desperate shortage of recruits, and perhaps additionally of the low quality of many conscripts from the provinces. Steadily, the Roman army became barbarized, as

---

[288] As we will see later, there have been many historians who have attributed the collapse of the empire that occurred between the fourth and fifth centuries to inadequacies on the part of the Roman military. Undoubtedly among them are Vegetius, a Roman historian, and Edward Gibbon.

[289] S. MacDowell, *Late Roman Infantryman 236-565 AD*, Reed Consumer Books, London, 1994, p. 11 and P. Erdkamp, *A Companion to the Roman Army*, Blackwell Publishing, 2007, pp. 516-517.

more and more of its officers and men were drawn from the uncivilized peoples, and in particular the German tribes.

These men had little reason to feel political or cultural loyalty to Rome.

The problem became worse with the growing use of the *foederati*, units in which barbarians served under their own tribal leaders rather than Roman officers. The Roman army is supposed to have decayed until it was a little more than a mass of mercenary warbands led by barbarian chieftains. This is sometimes held to have been a major factor in the collapse of the western Empire. (...) In the main our sources for the period do not appear to have seen this as a problem. Barbarian recruits were in general as loyal and efficient as any others, even when fighting against their own people. Occasionally, barbarian fighters turned traitor, but so in this period did some Romans. By the late 4th century, many senior officers were of barbarian descent, yet most of these men appear to have been culturally assimilated into the Roman military aristocracy. The belief that 'barbarisation' of the army contributed to the fall of Rome has now been largely discredited.[290]"

The Caesars made extensive use of barbarians in their ranks partly because of the demographic difficulties posed by the empire and partly because its inhabitants were hardly attracted to martial life. Leaving aside the pay (which we will discuss in more detail in the next paragraph), it can be said that the general conditions in which a soldier lived had improved since the time of the Principate. Roman soldiers could now get married and have a family while serving. A papyrus document found in Egypt reports that the daily military ration consisted of 1.3 kilograms of bread, approximately 1 kilogram of meat, 1 litre of wine and 70 centilitres of oil. It is indicative of the measures implemented by imperial actors to make the life of the Roman soldier more comfortable[291].

However, these efforts did not produce the desired results. Although from a later period than covered here in this work, the Theodosian code provides compelling evidence supporting the viewpoint that recruiting for the Roman army was immensely difficult. To avoid military service, many offered slaves in their place and some even

---

[290] A. Goldsworthy, *The Complete Roman Army*, Thames and Hudson, 2003, pp. 208-209.

[291] S. MacDowell, *Late Roman Infantryman 236-565 AD*, Reed Consumer Books, London, 1994, p. 18-19. For further details on the Roman military diet: R.W. Davies, "The Roman Military Diet", *Britannia*, Vol. 2 (1971), pp. 122-142.

mutilated themselves. For this reason, it should not be surprising that the military was filled with individuals from the *barbaricum* [292]. Following that, a crucial moment in the development of the army of Late Antiquity was the enactment of the *Constitutio Antoniniana* in 212, initiated by Caracalla. The provision guaranteed Roman citizenship to all the free inhabitants of the empire. Thus, the great division that had characterized the Principate's army came to an end. In fact, as the status of *peregrinus* disappeared (an inhabitant of a Roman province without citizenship) so too did the distinction between legionary troops and auxiliary troops[293]. The empire's dominance waned alongside the importance of the legion (which was constituted ethnically in large part by inhabitants of the peninsula and the provinces that had been established the longest).

Unofficially under Gallienus and officially under the Tetrarchy, the army incorporated a new division (*limitanei* and *comitatenses*) to meet the tactical-strategic mobility demands of the time. Sources report that the Roman army under Diocletian amounted to about 435,000 troops (390,000 in ground forces and 45,000 in various sea and river fleets)[294]. Some estimate that there was a 100% increase compared to previously recorded figures; however, this seems unlikely given the demographic and financial challenges that such an increase would have presented. New types of units were introduced while the old ones underwent significant modifications[295]. The legions of this period (280-305) increased from 39 to 59 but still had only about one quarter of the forces of the legions of the Principate[296], 1,500-2,000 units (all completely on foot) compared to 6,000[297].

---

[292] P. Erdkamp, *A Companion to the Roman Army*, Blackwell Publishing, 2007, p. 518-519.

[293] Ibidem, pp. 519-520.

[294] Ibidem, p. 517.

[295] Ibidem.

[296] E. C. Nischer, "The Army Reforms of Diocletian and Constantine and Their Modifications Up to the Time of the *Notitia Dignitatum*", *The Journal of Roman Studies*, Society for the Promotion of Roman Studies, Vol. 13 (1923), pp. 1-55.

[297] M. Rocco, *Persistenze e cesure nell'esercito romano dai Severi a Teodosio I: ricerche in ambito socio-politico, istituzionale, strategico*, University of Padua, pp. 152.

This was due to the widespread use of *vexillationes*, units that detached from the "mother legion" and did not rejoin it once they had fulfilled their military duties. This practice, already in use by the second century A.D., became more and more commonplace because of the policy of military mobility and flexibility promoted by Gallienus and his successors[298]. It revolutionized the legions, turning them into mobile units that were prudently placed near Roman borders. New units were then introduced, usually made up of fewer men than those during the Principate. There were the *scholae*[299], listed in the *Notitia Dignitatum* (written between the end of the fourth century and the beginning of the fifth century), which were composed of elite cavalry grouped into units of 500 men (in a certain sense similar to the old auxiliary *alae*). However, most of the military units consisted of *comitatenses* and *palatines*, whose individual units never exceeded 600 troops. The *comitatenses* were mobile troops stationed in areas near the border and commanded by the *duces* while the *palatines* (from Palatium, the hill where the imperial palace stood) were under the emperor's direct command[300]. Then there were the *pseudocomitatenses*[301], units that were originally composed of *limitanei* but later merged with the *comitati*. Even the command structure changed: among the many reforms carried out by Gallienus, one of the most important was filling the military command with men of equestrian rank rather than senatorial rank. At this point, Roman nobles were uninterested in *castrum* life, preferring to remain in the cities and enjoy a more luxurious lifestyle. Thus, the exclusively senatorial roles of *legatus legionis* and *tribunus laticlavus* disappeared, the former being the commander and the latter the deputy commander of the legion[302].

---

[298] K.R. Dixon, P. Southern, *Late Roman Army*, 1996, pp. 31-32.

[299] M. Rocco, *Persistenze e cesure nell'esercito romano dai Severi a Teodosio I: ricerche in ambito socio-politico, istituzionale, strategico*, University of Padua, pp. 233-236.

[300] G. Cascarino, C. Sansilvestri, *L'esercito romano, Armamento e organizzazione, Vol. III – Dal III secolo alla fine dell'Impero d'Occidente*, Il Cerchio, Rimini, 2009, pp. 29-69.

[301] Ibidem, p. 358.

[302] Aurelius Victor, *De Caesaribus*, 33, 33-34.

The *praefectus legionis* (of equestrian rank) became the new leading figure in the legion. A new class of military officers was thereby created, consisting mostly of men from the provinces who had spent their lives in the army. Gallienus' reform has been viewed by ancient historiography as a sign of hatred towards the senatorial class, but it was a necessary measure, among many others of this period, to better adapt the empire to the problematic conditions of the time. Diocletian brought further reforms. Almost all the units that were stationed on regional bases were entrusted to the *praefecti pretorio*, who were flanked by the *duces limitis* (border commanders)[303]. Given that the new Roman divisions were organized with fewer individuals, it followed that the ranks of the units changed, too. Analysis of these quantitative changes shows them to be impactful. As already noted, historians of Late Antiquity wrongly complain of a progressive "debasement" of the *miles romanus*.

Beginning with the Tetrarchy, a systematic change was made in Roman military structure, made possible thanks to the introduction of the *fabricae*, actual war equipment factories entirely under state control. They were located along the main roads and operated according to military commands.

"It is beginning from the age of Diocletian, in the last part of the third century A.D., the state-owned factories called *fabricae* began to work to supply clothing and armour directly to the army. Although private artisans continued to operate and serve the army, the creation of these factories secured necessary supplies for the war machine and avoided concerns such as those associated with exorbitant prices. As a result, the legions could more easily rely on supply chains and inventory. The workers of these state-owned factories were called *fabricenses* and were organized into an association called *corpus fabricensium* (...). About 40 *fabricae* were located in the eastern Mediterranean provinces, in Gaul, Illyria and Italy[304]."

---

[303] M. Rocco, *Persistenze e cesure nell'esercito romano dai Severi a Teodosio I: ricerche in ambito socio-politico, istituzionale, strategico*, University of Padua, pp. 278.

[304] R. Kroeze, A. Vitoria, G. Geltner, *Anti-corruption in History: From Antiquity to the Modern Era*, Oxford, 2017, p. 57.

This provision was adopted within the context of state streamlining imposed by Diocletian. When the empire reached a crisis, lacking financial, material and demographic resources, the tetrarchs considered it prudent to establish a centralized system of factories to implement standardized production of armaments. During the first two centuries of the empire, the equipment costs of the legionaries were automatically deducted from their pay. Their armour came partly from legionary workshops and partly from those of local artisans[305]. The Crisis of the Third Century, however, compromised the prevailing system of self-production of weapons, which made the army much more dependent on civil production than in the past. This was a situation that a military force under continuous strain like the Roman army was could not afford. Consequently, civil production suffered the devastating effects of inflation because the imperial administration, which was practically the only customer of the workshops, paid the craftsmen with money[306]. In order to keep the workshops producing the necessary goods, Diocletian decided to incorporate all of these production centres into a rigid and nationalized system. The *fabricae* were located on strategic sites, not far from Roman military hotspots on the Rhine and Danube, and in the Middle East[307]. These centres modified the basic equipment of Roman soldiers, in order to work within the stringent financial parameters of the state. As these factories spread during the time of the Tetrarchy, new types of head gear were developed. The highly refined but difficult to produce Gallic-type helmets were abandoned in favour of helmets that were simpler in design and better suited for mass production[308]. This change was almost certainly established by the Roman state.

---

[305] M. Rocco, *Persistenze e cesure nell'esercito romano dai Severi a Teodosio I: ricerche in ambito socio-politico, istituzionale, strategico*, University of Padua, pp. 167.
[306] Ibidem, pp. 168-170.
[307] Ibidem.
[308] Ibidem, pp. 173-175.

The artisans, now employed in the *fabricae*, no longer worked to accommodate the demands of the individual soldier but rather, the imperial authorities who wanted new pieces offering the same coverage as previous ones but also reduced costs and production times[309].

The arched helmet ("ridge helmet"), also known as the "Intercisa" (named after the Roman fort in present-day Hungary where the artifact was found), is an excellent example of the new military design introduced between the end of the third century and beginning of the fourth. Inspired by head gear used by their Sassanid enemies, these helmets were composed of two semi-metallic caps held together by a longitudinal iron crest, while the neck roll and the cheek pieces were kept attached with strips of leather[310]. The "Intercisa" was a simple and economical option. Although it was not as protective, it was part of an overall effort to reduce spending. Another piece of head gear produced in the empire's workshops was the "Spangenhelm", borrowed from the Sarmatians. Like the arched helmet, it also followed a rather basic design. It was composed of several pieces of segmented metal, held together by rivets and a metal strip[311].

Industrial production during the time of Diocletian also encompassed other components of the Roman soldier's equipment. Throughout the third century, military artisans tried to simplify the *lorica segmentata* since its production was problematically complex. Another version was created called the "Newstead" (named according to its the place of discovery in southern Scotland); however, it did not solve the problem[312]. The *segmentata* then fell into disuse because it required highly technical skills to produce and was costly both in terms of time and money. Evidently, the Roman war machine could not afford this. The *segmentata* was represented for the last time in imperial iconography at the beginning of the third century on the Arch of Septimius[313].

---

[309] Ibidem.
[310] Ibidem.
[311] Ibidem.
[312] A. Goldsworthy, *The Complete Roman Army*, Thames and Hudson, 2003, pp. 129.
[313] M. Rocco, *Persistenze e cesure nell'esercito romano dai Severi a Teodosio I: ricerche in am-*

Instead, the *fabricae* focused their productive efforts on the simplest crocheted armour (the *loricae hamatae*), which became the most widespread defensive garment among the troops (but not among selected units such as the *clibanarii* and officers). In his *Epitoma Rei Militaris* (fourth to fifth century), the aristocratic historian Vegetius is highly critical of the armour used by Roman soldiers during Late Antiquity.

"For despite progress in cavalry arms thanks to the example of the Goths, and the Alans and Huns, the infantry as is well-known go unprotected. From the founding of the City down to the time of the deified Gratian, the infantry army was equipped with both cataphracts and helmets. But upon the intervention of neglect and idleness field exercises ceased, and arms which soldiers rarely donned began to be thought heavy. So they petitioned the Emperor that they should hand in first the cataphracts, then helmets.[314]"

According to Vegetius, the Romans of the fourth century had forgotten about their past and abandoned an important military custom; that is, wearing armour. This discipline had once led the empire to dominate the world.

The reality, of course, was very different than what the moralistic narrative of the *Epitoma Rei Militaris* conveys. The Roman soldiers, as has already been said, mainly dressed in *loricae hamatae*, even after the Tetrachy. What is described by Vegetius as "neglect" was actually a tactical necessity. Many of the imperial troops during Late Antiquity spent most of their service in fixed locations. As such, it was customary for soldiers on patrol or watch, or during marches, to leave their armour at their bases[315]. There was also a profound change in offensive weapons, related to the previously mentioned homogenization of legionary and auxiliary troops.

bito socio-politico, istituzionale, strategico, University of Padua, pp. 85-88.

[314] Vegetius, *Epitoma Rei Militaris*, 1, 20.

[315] S. MacDowell, *Late Roman Infantryman 236-565 AD*, Reed Consumer Books, London, 1994, p. 16-17.

"On the other hand, there are now very few doubts about the fact that the legions as well as the old *auxilia* gravitated towards a single type of equipment between the second and third centuries, according to the writing of Tacitus, funerary sculptures of the first century A.D., reliefs adorning the Trajan Column and the metopes of the *Tropaeum Traiani* in Adamclisi. Until that time, distinctions between armaments had been functional. The *pilum* was an effective short-range impact weapon, which served to disrupt the enemy lines. The rectangular concave *scutum* ensured that the infantryman could defend themselves in close combat, in which case they struck with the squat *gladius*. This allowed them to remain protected by the shield much better than if maneuvering a long sword. The weapons of auxiliary infantry, on the other hand, including the *spatha*, *hasta* and flat oval shield, were effective in skirmishes in open formation as well as in combat on the front line, as demonstrated in the famous battle of *Mons Graupius* in A.D. 84[316]. In essence, the legionaries were unbeatable in a single type of combat, while the *auxiliaries could adapt to a greater number of different scenarios*, especially since they also employed archery units and a large cavalry.[317]"

The critique of Vegetius, who called for a return to the legion of before, was unwarranted. Archaeological findings from Late Antiquity testify to the use of armour. Even the literary sources such as the *Notitia Dignitatum* do not deny this. The *Notitia Dignitatum* reports the presence of various factories used for the production of helmets, shields and armour. Vegetius' thesis was based on reports about the lack of armour in the architectural reproductions of the time. However, this absence does not mean that armour had not been used in battle; rather, it probably points to a simplification in design[318]. The Romans decided to transform the army for purely functional purposes. External threats and the precarious internal situation required that the emperors create a well-armed yet economically sustainable force. The structure of the Augustan legions was completely inadequate for the defensive and offensive dynamics of the third and fourth centuries.

---

[316] The Battle of Mons Graupius took place on a still undefined site in northeastern Scotland between the Romans and a Caledonian tribe. During the battle the Roman commander Julius Agricola employed numerous units of *auxilia* in the melee.

[317] M. Rocco, *Persistenze e cesure nell'esercito romano dai Severi a Teodosio I: ricerche in ambito socio-politico, istituzionale, strategico*, University of Padua, pp. 83.

[318] Ibidem, p.84.

THE NEW LEGIONNAIRE
SINCE DIOCLETIAN'S MILITARY REFORMS
(late 3rd century - 5th century)

"INTERCISA" RIDGE HELMET
It is a low-cost head protection based on eastern helmets. The *Intercisa* type is characterized by a two-part bowl united by a central ridge running from front to back and small cheekpieces.

HASTA
It was a spear longer than the *pilum*. This weapon was not thrown, but was used for thrusting.

LORICA HAMATA
Armor composed by a thick mail made of metal rings. It was more comfortable and can last more without maintainance than the famous *lorica segmentata*.

CLIPEUS
Large round (or oval) shield used initially only by the cavalry. Late Antiquity finds and artworks indicate the use of *clipei* by foot soldiers. It could be dished or flat.

SPATHA
This sword, longer than the *gladius*, was probably of Germanic origin. During Late Roman Era, it became the service weapon of heavy infantry.

Legionary of Late Antiquity, also known as the "comitatensis".
Clearly, the previous armaments, consisting of the rectangular scutum, gladius and segmented lorica, were abandoned in favour of less expensive equipment better suited to the tactical demands of this period.

(© Davide Montingelli)

112

With this in mind, both the foot soldiers and the cavalry were equipped with the *spatha*[319], a cutting weapon used by the Germanic tribes. It was a sword much longer than the Roman *gladius* (between 75 and 100 centimetres in length approximately), guaranteeing greater offensive efficacy than its predecessor, being suitable for slashes and lunges[320]. The new weapon was held on the left by the Roman soldiers, due to its length and likely because the *scutum*, the typical rectangular legionary shield had been abandoned. It was abandoned in favour of smaller, circular shields, while the *pila* were replaced by *lanceae*, javelins that were much longer than their predecessors[321].

In contrast to what Gibbon and Vegetius thought, the appearance of the *miles*, the basic private level foot soldier, changed dramatically. The quality of the protective gear was not necessarily made poorer; it was instead, modified to meet field requirements. Obviously, the Roman army suffered very serious defeats during Late Antiquity, but the same can also be said about the empire at its height. Those defeats after Diocletian were in large part due to the chaos in the empire, rather than the result of the alleged barbarization of the units. When the Romans were not plagued by deficiencies in the chain of command, they often succeeded in winning battles. The Battle of Satala (298), one of the greatest victories recorded by the Romans against the Sassanids, was mentioned in previous chapters. The Battle of Strasbourg (356) and the Battle of Solicinium (368) and Argentaria (378) are also worthy of note. This is because, despite what has been handed down by certain historiographies, Roman superiority in terms of discipline and logistics persisted well into the empire's later periods.

---

[319] Ibidem, p. 86.

[320] Ammianus Marcellinus, *History*, 31, 7, 14. The historian from Late Antiquity reports that a stroke from the *spatha* could cut a human skull in two.

[321] J. C. N. Coulston, "How to Arm a Roman Soldier", *Bulletin of the Institute of Classical Studies. Supplement*, Wiley, No. 71 (1998), p. 181.

From infantry to cavalry

Even well before the third century, the Roman army faced many difficulties confronting enemies who utilized troops on horseback as their main offense. Significant changes were needed, even at a tactical level. The cohort and century had partly lost the versatility of the past, since they were composed exclusively of heavy infantry[322] (the variety during the time of the Republic generated by the differentiation between *hastati, triarii* and *principes* could not be matched by the auxiliary troops in the Imperial Age). The role of the infantry was thus profoundly modified. The troops on foot returned to a basic formation, the phalanx[323]. Caracalla and Alexander Severus had made this choice in the past. The former had transformed the *Legio II Parthica* into a unit very similar to those used by Alexander the Great in his Asian campaign (the *pezhetairoi*)[324] while the latter had utilized the phalanx in uniting 6 legions into a single force[325].

The ideal phalanx formation, according to the *Strategikon* of Maurice, Byzantine emperor (sixth century), was composed of no less than 4 rows and no more than 16. Probably the most commonly used number of rows was 8, which allowed the unit to hit hard and remain flexible[326]. Once the battle had begun each row had a different task. The most exposed also wore the most armour and formed a wall with their shields. By contrast, the soldiers positioned further back were outfitted with lighter armour and were charged with striking the enemy with throwing weapons like javelins or arrows. Even the cavalry underwent great changes. Despite Rome's long-standing reluctance to utilize this type of unit, even Julius Caesar had understood the importance of cavalry, recruiting thousands of *equites* among the Germans and Gauls

---

[322] M. Rocco, *Persistenze e cesure nell'esercito romano dai Severi a Teodosio I: ricerche in ambito socio-politico, istituzionale, strategico*, University of Padua, pp. 89-90.

[323] S. MacDowell, *Late Roman Infantryman 236-565 AD*, Reed Consumer Books, London, 1994, p. 30.

[324] Herodian, *History of the Roman Empire Since the Death of Marcus Aurelius*, 4, 9, 4.

[325] Historia Augusta, *Alexander Severus*, 60, 5.

[326] Ibidem.

for his army. It was mainly through contact with two specific peoples that the emperors came to understand that cavalry could be an excellent instrument of war: the Parthians, who had killed 30,000 legionaries in the Battle of Carrhae with light cavalry[327], and the Sarmatians. The latter clashed for the first time with the Romans in the sixties of the first century A.D. when they attracted the attention of the imperial military commanders with a series of raids in modern-day Bulgaria[328]. In that episode, the Sarmatian contingent was easily wiped out by a single legion; however, the armament used by the barbarians did not go unnoticed by Tacitus.

"But as on this occasion the day was damp and the ice thawed, what with the continual slipping of their horses, and the weight of their coats of mail, they could make no use of their pikes or their swords, which being of an excessive length they wield with both hands. These coats are worn as defensive armour by the princes and most distinguished persons of the tribe. They are formed of plates of iron or very tough hides, and though they are absolutely impenetrable to blows...[329]"

Despite the clumsy manoeuvring and the lack of shields described in a disparaging manner by the Roman historian, these horsemen constituted a threat beyond the Danube. During the campaigns launched in the area by Trajan, the units on horseback became increasingly important, acquiring many of these "exogenous" characteristics. The Trajan Column clearly testifies that the *numeri* and *alae* increased in quantity and became more specialized[330]. It was Hadrian, however, who created the first truly "impenetrable" unit with the *Ala I Gallorum et Pannoniorum catafracta*. This unit partly resulted from the expertise of the *contarii* introduced by Vespasian and the

---

[327] The Battle of Carrhae was one of the most bitter defeats in Roman military history. It proved that in open field battle the heavy infantry could not cope with a substantial light cavalry force, without also having a large contingent on horseback.

[328] J.W. Eadie, "The Development of Roman Mailed Cavalry", *The Journal of Roman Studies*, Vol. 57, No. 1-2. (1967), p. 165.

[329] Tacitus, *Histories*, 1, 79, 1.

[330] J.W. Eadie, "The Development of Roman Mailed Cavalry", *The Journal of Roman Studies*, Vol. 57, No. 1-2. (1967), p. 166-167.

example presented by the Sarmatic and Parthian cataphracted knights[331]. When Gallienus came to power these types of units were multiplied, not only because of his choosing but also because the *clibanarii*, the Sassanid armoured cavalry, appeared in the eastern battlefields. The Romans learned to respect these heavy units and, in turn, developed other similar units between the end of the third century and the beginning of the fourth century, while still preferring the cataphracts. These soldiers on horseback were in fact less heavily armoured and more mobile manoeuvring than the *clibanarii*, who were only suitable for a *charge à fond*, which is to say, a head-on attack[332]. Despite its growing importance, the cavalry continued to play a subordinate role in the infantry. While the infantry fought the "real" battle, the troops on horseback attempted to encircle the enemy through a series of short skirmishes with the enemy cavalry[333]. Despite what some may think, the army troops of Late Antiquity were rigorously trained (the *protectores* were usually the officers assigned to this task) and were able to execute a variety of formations, even under the mental and physical pressures that the battles could create[334]. The tactics used from the Diocletian age onwards were clearly more defensive than those of the Principate. Roman troops tended to avoid, if possible, head-on collisions, which was unlike how they fought in the past[335]. This is not because the army had become less competent, as many have claimed in various historical accounts (it has already been shown that the Romans won numerous battles at this time just as they did at the height of the empire) but rather, to avoid losses which, due to demographics at the time, would have been difficult to replace[336].

---

[331] Ibidem, p. 167.

[332] Ibidem, pp. 168-170.

[333] Ibidem, p.171. Even during Late Antiquity, the role of the calvary never dominated the tactical choices of Roman commanders. During the Battle of Strasbourg (356), the Roman heavy cavalry was the first unit to engage, risking the rest of the imperial troops lagging behind.

[334] S. MacDowell, *Late Roman Infantryman 236-565 AD*, Reed Consumer Books, London, 1994, p. 11.

[335] Ibidem, pp. 30-45.

[336] Ibidem.

The Roman calvary pursuing the Sarmatians on a segment of Trajan's Column.
Note the armour of the calvary from the steppes.
(© Wikicommons/Conrad Cichorius)

Troops from Late Antiquity abandoned the "honour" mentality which was very much a part of the Republican and Imperial eras. It disapproved of those who secretly attacked by ambush or quick encirclement, types of engagement now accepted by the Roman command[337].

During the Principate, legions launched several rounds of *pila* to upset enemy units before throwing themselves head-on into bloody clashes in which Roman soldiers almost always had the upper hand because of their technological superiority (namely in armour and weapons). Before the charge, archers and slingers added to the damage done by the *pila*[338]. In Late Antiquity, throwing weapons and mounted troops were employed in the same way but how infantry was used changed considerably. Units on foot waited for the enemy, equipped with spears 2.5 metres in length, which passed through spaces in the shape of a 'V' formed by circular helmets. This formation, called *fulcum*, was clearly a development of the *testudo* formation[339]. In general, however, the imperial forces at that time favoured small-scale skirmishes to large-scale confrontations. For this reason, as well as the incredible speed of their operations, they avoided wearing armour. It is useful to note that even these war tactics reflected, in a certain sense, the streamlining of this period. The goal was to inflict the most damage possible while suffering the least number of losses. An example of this tactical mentality was the Battle of Strasbourg. During the battle, the Alemanni converged several times on the Roman camp but the soldiers, holding strong behind their shield wall, were able to resist for a long time, causing serious losses to the barbarians. On that occasion, victory was achieved through tactically waiting and wearing down the enemy which, in the long run, forced the Alemanni to make unsustainable offensive efforts.

---

[337] Ibidem, pp. 45-47.

[338] Ibidem.

[339] For further information on the *fulcum*: P. Rance, "The Fulcum, the Late Roman and Byzantine Testudo: the Germanization of Roman Infantry Tactics?", *Greek, Roman, and Byzantine Studies*, 44 (2004), pp. 265-326.

"The Alemanni were stronger and taller, our soldiers disciplined by long practice; they were savage and uncontrollable, our men quiet and wary, these relying on their courage, while the Germans presumed upon their huge size. (...) And so there suddenly leaped forth a fiery band of nobles, among whom even the kings fought, and with the common soldiers following they burst in upon our lines before the rest; and opening up a path for themselves they got as far as the legion of the Primani, which was stationed in the centre (...) there our soldiers, closely packed and in fully-manned lines, stood their ground fast and firm, like towers, and renewed the battle with greater vigour; and being intent upon avoiding wounds, they protected themselves like murmillos, and with drawn swords pierced the enemy's sides, left bare by their frenzied rage. But the enemy strove to lavish their lives for victory and kept trying to break the fabric of our line (...). But when they heard the frequent groans of the dying, they were overcome with panic and lost their courage. Worn out at last by so many calamities, and now being eager for flight alone, over various paths they made haste with all speed to get away...[340]"

The Roman soldiers probably tried to "indulge" the barbaric *cuneus* (triangular formation aimed at breaking the opposing side's first line) with the *forfex*, a 'V' formation that met the barbaric horde and then closed around it in a pincer grip[341]. The concept of *res militaris*, which matured in the aftermath of the Crisis of the Third Century, was thus profoundly changed in comparison with the past, although it should not be considered, as already discussed, less effective.

Changes to taxation and currency

The Roman economy was supported for centuries thanks to the great achievements of its armies. During the Republican Age, the victories of the legions guaranteed numerous slaves (which formed the backbone of the workforce in the ancient world) and huge resources of various kinds. Economic estimates made in recent times say that Rome's gross domestic product during the time of Augustus was very close to that of Holland and England before they became dominant

---

[340] Ammianus Marcellinus, *Histories*, 16, 12, 47-51.
[341] Aulus Gellius, *Attic Nights*, 10, 9.

powers in the modern age (between the sixteenth and seventeenth centuries)[342]. Other studies say that it approached the gross domestic product of the Eastern Empire in the year 1000 and of India immediately after the Second World War[343]. Unlike what was said in the past by some rather pessimistic scholars, who believed that economic growth was the exclusive prerogative of the Industrial Age, the Roman economy was not as stagnant as others in the ancient world.

"The decreasing price of naval transport allowed production to be allocated around the Mediterranean, where conditions were more favorable. Instead of using wheat grown in Italy, the inhabitants of Rome ate soups and bread made from wheat grown in Sicily, Egypt, Africa, Spain and other places. Production was spread out because it was cheaper to grow wheat in these places than in Italy (...). Trade, which allowed regions to specialize in what they produced best, increased the revenue of both the regions that sent goods and those that received them. Trade functioned as an extension of resources in each region; it loosened the constraint of limited land in an agricultural economy like the Roman one. One of the effects of Roman regional specialization was the change made by Italian farms, which replaced wheat with other types of crops that could not be cultivated elsewhere (...). Naval transport and roads both promoted a better life for Roman citizens; they allowed the creation of an urban society that was unique in the ancient world. The agricultural system, including agriculture, trade and related institutions, was efficient enough to free many people from food production. These people could gather in the cities and produce other goods and services. These added products improved the quality of Roman life and the per capita income.[344]"

Although it did not have the positive economic characteristics of early industrial Europe, at the beginning of its history the empire was pervaded by a general sense of well-being. Urbanization grew at an unprecedented rate, facilitated by architectural and technological progress that allowed the provision and storage of large quantities of water, necessary for the development of large inhabited settlements.

---

[342] W. Scheidel, S.J. Friesen, "The Size of the Economy and the Distribution of Income in the Roman Empire", *The Journal of Roman Studies*, Society for the Promotion of Roman Studies, Vol. 99 (2009), p. 64.

[343] Ibidem, pp. 72-73.

[344] P. Temin, *The Roman Market Economy*, Princeton University Press, 2013, pp. 222-223.

Complex societies developed in cities (although largely segmented) where literacy spread. It was not until the nineteenth century that it spread as fast again throughout Europe[345]. Further economic activity was promoted and legalized by public institutions. However, already in the second century, once the wars of conquest were over, the situation changed again. The economy was increasingly burdened by the large quantities of wheat required by the capital (on average 30 million *modii*, more than 200 tons of wheat per year[346]) and above all, the great costs of the Roman war machine. Consequently, the emperors began to address the situation.

Taxation

Initially, the heavy burden of military expenditures was partly supported by the *annona* (grain) system. The army could take whatever it needed from the population, which was in turn adequately reimbursed by imperial funds (the *fiscus*) [347]. The military salary consisted of more than money. A document on papyrus found in Egypt details the sums deducted from the pay of a Roman centurion during the reign of Titus (A.D. 79-81): his *stipendium* included meals, shoes, stockings and the *Saturnalia*, a famous festival in the Latin-speaking world[348].

In situations of extreme need, the army could rely on the *indictiones*, extraordinary requisitions, which the state eventually reimbursed (the emperor or wealthy citizens often paid directly). Although the *indictiones* were a serious inconvenience to local populations, especially during

---

[345] T. Frank, *An Economic History of Rome* (1927) Batoche Books Limited, 2004, pp. 182-197.

[346] Ibidem.

[347] R. I. Frank, "Ammianus on Roman Taxation", *The American Journal of Philology*, The Johns Hopkins University Press Vol. 93, No. 1, Studies in Honor of Henry T. Rowell (Jan., 1972), pp. 70.

[348] B. Campbell, *The Roman Army, 31 BC – AD 337: A Sourcebook* (1994), Routledge, London, 2006, pp. 23-24.

major campaigns, the system could have worked even more efficiently if the military and provincial authorities had coordinated [349]. Intensification of enemy activity inside and outside the empire required an ever-increasing effort to produce rations. Further aggravating the situation were imperial policies. Beginning with Septimius Severus, Roman troops were given various benefits, including free food rations [350]. During this period (probably under Caracalla) military provisions stopped being withheld from soldiers and it became the responsibility of the citizens to provide them. The transformation of the *annona* into a military necessity accelerated under the last of the Severi, Alexander. To prepare for the campaign against Ardashir, the emperor needed provisions in the form of food supplies for approximately 150,000 men. In order to obtain optimal control of grain transport and supply lines from Egypt to Mesopotamia, a *dux* was named who joined the civil administration officials of the provinces concerned[351]. The collection of the *annona* was carried out by *principales* and *actuarii* [352], legionary soldiers (but also auxiliaries) who had administrative and managerial duties in their units. As aforementioned, as anarchy infiltrated the military, the requisitions became increasingly more frequent and were reimbursed less often[353].

It was the Tetrarchy that is credited with formalizing and "civilizing" this system. The *annona militaris* became a genuine and regular tribute, whose collection was the responsibility of the vice prefects of the Praetorium and governors of the provinces who were free to manage the civil aspects of their territories without worrying about border defense, now entrusted to the *duces*[354].

---

[349] R. I. Frank, "Ammianus on Roman Taxation", *The American Journal of Philology*, The Johns Hopkins University Press Vol. 93, No. 1, Studies in Honor of Henry T. Rowell (Jan., 1972), pp. 70.

[350] Ibidem, p.71.

[351] F. Carlà, "Tu tantum praefecti mihi studium et annonam in necessariis locis praebe: prefettura al pretorio e annona militaris nel III secolo d. C.", *Historia: Zeitschrift für Alte Geschichte*, Franz Steiner Verlag, Bd. 56, H. 1 (2007), p. 12.

[352] Ibidem, pp. 17-18.

[353] Ibidem.

[354] Ibidem, p. 3.

The collection duties were entrusted to the *optiones*, individuals who straddled the military and civil worlds, and to the *tesserarii*. During the time of Diocletian, the latter became civil officials (at the height of the empire they were non-commissioned officers), working specifically at the municipal level, in charge of requisitioning food supplies and other general goods required by the army[355]. Likewise, "classic" positions in the Roman military apparatus were transformed. For example, the *primus pilus*, probably already in charge of legionary provisions at the height of the empire, became a position linked to the *annona*, starting from Septimius Severus. This is how the *primipile lustrum* was born, precisely from this position. Under Diocletian they became real civil officers, classified in urban cohorts[356]. The *frumentarii* disappeared instead. These were soldiers used for various tasks such as espionage, patrolling and delivering supplies (as can be deduced from their title). Their intelligence work was eventually taken over by the *agentes in rebus*, who did not have a "food" role, however[357]. All these changes were due to the Tetrarchy's general *leitmotiv*, which was separating the civil from the military which, due to the contingencies of the third century, had often been overlapping. The last position to be affected by the reform plan was the one filled by the *mensores*, who during the Principate were part of the military units and were in charge of the distribution of wheat and grain in the camps. From the beginning of the fourth century the *mensores* became civil servants in the *horrea*, the public granaries of the Roman Empire[358].

Returning to taxation, in addition to the formalization of the *annona militaris*, Diocletian established a rather innovative tax: the *capitatio-iugatio*.

---

[355] Ibidem, pp. 19-21.
[356] Ibidem, pp. 21-24.
[357] Ibidem, pp. 24-27.
[358] Ibidem, pp. 27-28.

"To deal with the financial crisis, Diocletian carried out a tax reform, recognizing the *iugum* (land extension) as a fiscal unit, hence the term *iugatio* (taxable land). In sources we find the *capitatio* mentioned alongside the *iugatio*, the former being a fairly controversial term indicating a personal tax, which affects the caput; that is, the person. It was therefore a mixed tax system, royal and personal (*iugatio-capitatio*). The taxable amount was not ascertained officially but was rather based on the declaration of the taxable person to which appropriate corrections were applied. The taxable age was established as the age of puberty which was fourteen years old for men and twelve years old for women. An important aspect of the Diocletian tax reform was the extension of the royal tax to the Italic funds, until then exempt. This resulted in the empire equating these funds with provincial ones and, from the point of view of the private institutions, represented a decisive step on the road to unification of various forms of real estate *dominium*, or more precisely of ownership.[359]"

In essence, this new "combined" tribute was imposed on people and on land that could be worked. The new system, which rested on new administrative divisions of *dioceses*, was made possible only following a census of the empire's inhabitants and taxable land. The value of the *iuga* and *capita* was not fixed. The differences were determined in various ways from *diocese* to *diocese*. Each *diocese* was in turn divided into provinces. Other important variables taken into account were the *numerus hominum*, the fertility of arable land and state need[360]. The required quota could fluctuate, even from one year to the next, since estimates were not typically made ahead of time (in ancient Rome there were no budgets and taxes were established yearly). For this reason, those who paid the taxes often found themselves in a difficult situation, since they did not know precisely what sum they would have had to pay[361]. The measure tied many peasants to their land, as taxes were often paid in kind, with agricultural goods. This new tax was applied throughout the empire, with the exception of some areas in Egypt, North Africa and Gaul[362].

---

[359] G. Franciosi, *Corso storico istituzionale di diritto romano*, Giappichelli, February 2015, pp. 217-218.

[360] A.H.M. Jones, "Capitatio and Iugatio", *The Journal of Roman Studies*, Society for the Promotion of Roman Studies, Vol. 47, No. 1/2 (1957), p. 88-94.

[361] Ibidem.

[362] Ibidem.

Even with the new fiscal measure in effect, the pragmatism of Diocletian is still obvious. There were already some forms of direct taxation in the empire, such as the *tributum capitis*, a personal tax on all inhabitants of the empire (except those who lived on the Italian peninsula), and the *tributum soli*, a percentage of the estimated value of the land.

The system devised by the emperor was, on the one hand, innovative because it created a new tax base, which was guaranteed by means of a census of the population and land. On the other hand, it introduced the *iugum*, a unit of measurement that allowed estimations of varying land types (instead of using the currency that at this time was very changeable).[363] Precisely because of the issue with the currency's devaluation, Diocletian decided to merge *capita* and *iuga*. Given the situation, it would have been much easier to obtain tributes in kind rather than in the form of money. The Diocletian reform implemented an equitable distribution of fiscal burdens, based on the productivity of the various workers of the empire or rather, on the productivity of the various lands in relation to the number of workers.[364]

The taxes were certainly burdensome, but the general context in which they were introduced must be understood. The four emperors had initiated a series of construction projects (palaces, roads, fortifications etc.) which incorporated more workers into the state machine. In essence, the inhabitants of the empire were burdened by new fiscal obligations of the *iugatio-capitatio*; however, they were also provided with the work necessary to meet them. What was collected by the tax system was immediately reinvested and thus returned, in the form of services, to the tax payers.

---

[363] Ibidem.
[364] Ibidem.

Against inflation

The regularization of the Roman monetary system was included in Octavian Augustus' reform program following the civil wars. As detailed in preceding paragraphs, the first Roman emperor had to bear innumerable expenses. Costs were incurred when veterans retired, which detracted from Octavian's plans for *Pax Romana* and investments aimed at reinvigorating the Italian peninsula[365]. Infighting had caused a money shortage since the many armies employed in previous years had to be handsomely paid.

For this reason, the *princeps* decided to bring order to the monetary system by stabilizing it and the value of its coins. The gold coin (*aureus*) would be equal to 25 silver coins (*denarii*), 100 orichalcum coins (*sestertii*) and 400 copper coins (*asses*)[366]. The precious metals in the *aureus* and *denarius*, the two most prominent coins, were almost pure. The first coin's weight was 7.79 grams (1/42 of a pound) while the second's was 3.89 grams (1/84 of a pound)[367]. The Augustan reform was a success and large amounts of coins circulated again throughout the empire. Job opportunities increased and prices started to rise again after a period of deflation that had begun in the late Republican era. All this was possible because of the activity of the Iberian mines and the booty collected in Egypt after Actium. Augustus was thus as capable in economic matters as he was in military ones even though he did not have much knowledge in this area (not unlike other Romans). The bimetallic system remained stable until Nero found himself fighting deflation again. The emperor decided to improve economic circumstances by depreciating coins produced with precious metals. The *aureus* fell in value approximately 11% and hit a weight of 7.27 grams (1/45 of a pound)[368].

---

[365] T. Frank, *An Economic History of Rome* (1927) Batoche Books Limited, 2004, pp. 182-197.

[366] A. Savio, *Monete Romane*, Jouvence, 2002, pp. 153-157.

[367] Ibidem.

[368] Pliny the Elder, *Natural History*, 33.

The *denarius* fell approximately 12.5% to 3.41 grams (1/96 of pound). Of note is that for the latter the intrinsic value was lowered due to its silver content, which decreased from 97% to 93.5%[369]. The reform was a success and Rome began to prosper again. Numerous public works were built (the Domus Aurea, namely) and large donations of money and grain were granted to the capital's population. Ancient historians tell us that the silver mines of Spain were very productive during this time as well as the gold mines of Illyria. However, a problem was festering that Neronian reforms could not fully address. The price of silver was rising due to the ever-increasing demand for money. Many *denarii* were required for Roman military undertakings at the borders while many others ended up in foreign markets, India being one example, in exchange for luxury goods. For this reason, Nero devalued the *denarius* more than the *aureus* in order to maintain the balance between the two most valuable currencies within the monetary system. Therefore, when we consider the devaluations made in the subsequent years by various emperors, we should not exclusively think of them as a fast way to generate money, as many have suggested in the past, but rather a way to maintain monetary equilibrium[370]. It is not by chance that the devaluations implemented by Trajan, Antoninus Pius and Marcus Aurelius were never implemented in periods of severe crisis (except those of Marcus Aurelius during the Marcomannic Wars). The oldest coins, which were also the ones with the highest silver content, did not immediately disappear, as devaluation measures were implemented slowly and quietly[371] [372].

---

[369] K. Butcher, *Debasement and the Decline of Rome*, pp. 190.

[370] A. Wassink, "Inflation and Financial Policy under the Roman Empire to the Price Edict of 301 A.D.", *Historia: Zeitschrift für Alte Geschichte*, Franz Steiner Verlag, Bd. 40, H. 4 (1991), p. 476-477.

[371] Ibidem.

[372] A. Savio, *Monete Romane*, Jouvence, 2002, pp. 171.

The situation began to deteriorate more rapidly starting from the end of the second century A.D., most likely facilitated by the Antonine Plague. Commodus greatly devalued the *denarius* to manage this situation (it went down to around 70% silver content)[373]. One of the main consequences of this measure was that the 1:25 ratio was completely distorted. The reform of Septimius Severus was aimed at resolving this problem in a coherent way as well at political legitimacy. The native emperor of Leptis Magna also drastically devalued the *denarius*, dropping the percentage of silver to around 60-50%[374]. Surely it was a measure driven by the need for more liquidity, but it cannot be denied that the intention was to replicate the success of the Augustan reform. Septimius Severus probably wanted to transform the *denarius* into a fiduciary currency, like Octavian did with the *sestertius*[375], which in the Republican Age was made of silver; part of the provision included penalties for those who demanded more than 25 *denarii* in exchange for an *aureus*. Under these circumstances, large quantities of coins were issued. They were used for public works, welfare and obviously, the army, which supported imperial power [376] . As aforementioned, the Severian reform had positive effects in the short term (certainly helped by the gold plundered at Ctesiphon), but failed to transform the *denarius* into a fiduciary currency, since the 1:25 ratio with the *aureus* was by this time completely distorted.

Caracalla carried out another reform and was successful where his father had failed. He reduced the weight of the *aureus* from 7.2 grams to 6.5 grams and introduced a new silver coin (aimed at replacing the old *denarius*), which would have respected the ratio 1:25 with the *aureus*[377]. However, the reform was not fully completed, and indeed for many scholars, it marked the beginning of the end of the Roman monetary system.

---

[373] Ibidem.
[374] Ibidem, p. 478.
[375] Ibidem.
[376] Ibidem, p. 479.
[377] Ibidem, p. 480.

"Mommsen identified Caracalla's new coin as the one that precipitated the crisis. Although its weight and fineness suggested it was worth one-and-a-half denarii, as earlier scholars had proposed, he argued that it was 'ein binio oder Doppeldenar'. It was thus a form of debasement, albeit one that did not involve reducing the fineness. He also argued that it could not have been called a *denarius*, and proposed two other possible names, both taken from the *Historia Augusta*: 'aurelianus' or 'antoninianus'. Neither name is regarded as credible today, but the latter one stuck, while the term 'aurelianus' is now applied to the reformed radiates of Aurelian and his successors. In spite of modern scholarly attempts to rebrand the coin as a 'radiate', Mommsen's 'antoninianus' remains common currency. The new coin thus took centre stage in the account of the collapse of the Roman monetary system. Its introduction by Caracalla had signified a major debasement but subsequent reductions in fineness reduced its value still further. Proof that it was heavily overvalued could be adduced from the number of contemporary forgeries. Not only was quality to blame, but quantity too: for Mommsen, the huge size of *antoninianus* hoards illustrated the oversupply of currency and its general worthlessness.[378]"

The problem was that this *antoninianus* was intrinsically worth 1.5 *denarii*, and not two as was stated by the imperial authority. The new currency thus failed to replace the *denarius* (although it was reintroduced by Balbinus and Pupienus in order to have a coin with greater value to pay for their war with Maximinus Thrax)[379]. This reform contributed to undermining the population's confidence in a system that had already lost much credibility with the depreciations of past years.

After Caracalla there were few sovereigns that had the time to worry about inflation problems in the medium to long term. The numerous emperors that emerged in the third century dealt exclusively with stimulating funds to feed the war machine. The sums requested by the military were in fact always greater. The value of *stipendia* and *donativa* shot up exponentially and with time came to represent almost the entire public expenditure of the Roman state.

Indeed, an analysis of Roman economic problems would be incomplete without a clear picture of the extent of per capita military supplies of the imperial army.

---

[378] K. Butcher, *Debasement and the Decline of Rome*, pp. 188.
[379] Ibidem, pp. 190-191.

As for the legionaries, under Augustus the annual salary stood at 225 *denarii*. The 120 *equites* alongside the legion drew 1/6 more than the legionary infantry, up to about 260 *denarii*[380]. In this period, a centurion could be paid eighteen times more than a common soldier. He could earn 3,375 *denarii*, while the *primus pilus* received a whopping 13,500[381]. In A.D. 84, Domitian granted an increase up to 300 *denarii* (in three instalments that individually ranged from 75 to 100 *denarii*)[382]. A further increase occurred under Septimius Severus in A.D. 197 when the emperor increased wages by 50%; his son Caracalla followed suit with an increase of the same percentage[383]. The last to increase the total wages before the tetrarchical reorganization was Maximinus Thrax, who doubled the figures received by the soldiers. Under his rule a *primus pilus* came to collect 108,000 *denarii* annually[384]! The emperors of the third century, on the other hand, could not think of anything other than preserving their power, through considerable donations.

But meanwhile the system declined. The oldest *denarii*, and therefore the least debased, were gradually withdrawn from the market due to Gresham's Law, which surely must have caused a collapse of the economic-financial system, given that the anchor currency of the monetary system, as it had been conceived by Augustus, actually disappeared. The *denarii* minted under Gordian III contained 1.46 grams of silver, while under Gallienus and Claudius II (Claudius Gothicus) they came to contain 0.16 grams and 0.10 to 0.04 grams, respectively[385]. An economy that could once be defined as monetary now transformed into one where coins made way for a new currency: payment in kind.

---

[380] P. Erdkamp, *A Companion to the Roman Army*, Blackwell Publishing, 2007, p. 308-309.

[381] Ibidem.

[382] P.I. Prodromídis, *Another View on an Old Inflation: Environment and Policies in the Roman Empire up to Diocletian's Price Edict*, Centre of Planning and Economic Research, Athens, February 2006, p. 13.

[383] Ibidem.

[384] P. Erdkamp, *A Companion to the Roman Army*, Blackwell Publishing, 2007, p. 308.

[385] K. Butcher, *Debasement and the Decline of Rome*, pp. 184.

The first to try to circumvent this undesirable situation was Aurelian. The *Restaurator Orbis* did all that he could to reorganize since the empire had been divided for years and had been showing economic cracks for some time. First, Aurelian established what would have been officially authorized mints[386]: Mediolanum-Ticinum (strategically placed near the command of mobile cavalry stationed there), Viminacium, Trier, Antioch, Serdica, Siscia and Cizico, Alexandria and Lugdunum (the latter added only after the reconquest of Palmyra and the Gauls). They were reorganized as imperial mints like the ones in Rome, which by now had an overwhelming supply flow.

"With the reform of A.D. 274, Aurelian also initiated a drastic rearrangement of the empire's 540 mints. Only 10 remained, organized into different workshops. Continuing the policy of Claudius, all the mints had to abandon extensive local production of bronze so as to adopt a single currency. This was what Rome's mint issued, which meant that Rome once again became the monetary centre of the empire where people communicated using only the Latin language. The only exception was Alexandria in Egypt, which continued the production of the tetradrachm, with legends in Greek, although its weight was reduced with increasingly cheap alloys.[387]"

Aurelian then moved on to the actual coins. He returned the weight of the *aureus* to 6.5 grams (before it was 5.54 grams) and issued a new coin, the double *aureus*, which depicted an effigy of the emperor in person and had an average weight of 8.25 grams[388]. However, the most innovative feature of the Aurelian reforms concerned a new "nominal" silver coin (actually made of silver-finished bronze containing 4 to 5% silver), which weighed 3.9 grams and bore the trademark "XXI".

---

[386] A. Wassink, "Inflation and Financial Policy under the Roman Empire to the Price Edict of 301 A.D.", *Historia: Zeitschrift für Alte Geschichte*, Franz Steiner Verlag, Bd. 40, H. 4 (1991), p. 484.

[387] R. Diegi, "Le monete di Aureliano", *Panorama numismatico*, n° 251/maggio 2010, p. 12.

[388] A. Wassink, "Inflation and Financial Policy under the Roman Empire to the Price Edict of 301 A.D.", *Historia: Zeitschrift für Alte Geschichte*, Franz Steiner Verlag, Bd. 40, H. 4 (1991), p. 484-485.

This trademark indicated the value relationship between this new silver/antoninian (many call it *aurelianus*) and the *aureus*. Effectively, 20 of these coins had the same value as a single gold coin[389].

"The reform of 274 was deflationary and, at the same time, inflationary. The aureus was depreciated in terms of bronze, but given that the monetary circulation was practically based on silver-finished gold-bronze bimetallism, the latter was elevated to the status of silver. The reform was also inflationary due to the fiduciary character of the currency that was worth much more than it contained in precious metal. The state proceeded with the withdrawal of old coins, which by now no longer inspired confidence in the people, given their impoverished content and decidedly poor appearance. The aurei, except for their extremely variable weight, were still a good-quality alloy. In addition, the *antoniniani* of Claudius II were already issued in silver-finished bronze, which increased their value. A real reform had to involve the disappearance of all the coins circulating previously and so it was done. (...) His monetary reform, which was certainly not only aimed at restoring Antonine dignity and beauty, as is often claimed perhaps in an unconsciously reductive manner, was highly effective because it materially touched all the citizens of the empire. A single type of currency had emerged, which had been carefully executed and made to look acceptable. It supplanted the enormous variety of bronze coins produced by peripheral mints and decorated with the Greek language. Latin had become, with the only temporary exception being Alexandria, the official language of all imperial coinage. Rome, with its customs and its language, resumed its existence even if only for a few decades, although Aurelian could not have imagined it, as the real political and monetary centre of the Empire.[390]"

Despite several merits acknowledged above, this reform also failed to be effective in the medium to long term. Aurelian was assassinated just one year after the introduction of the new system. Unfortunately for the empire, there were no longer the large amounts of precious metals as there had been in the past to support the monetary system. The last mines in operation, located in Dacia, were abandoned during these years for strategic and military purposes, which we underlined earlier. The silver and gold available were used in ever greater quantities to finance military efforts in defense of borders.

---

[389] Ibidem.

[390] R. Diegi, "Le monete di Aureliano", *Panorama numismatico*, n° 251/May 2010, pp. 12-14.

The monetary system was soon subjected to the debasement of the *denarius* and Roman troops had to resort to systematic terrorism and plunder of provincial populations to obtain the necessary supplies[391]. This accelerated the disappearance of coins in circulation and the increasing use of basic necessities in economic transactions.

The Diocletian monetary reform occurred in this context. The creator of the Tetrarchy intervened with the gold coin, which was renamed *solidus*, hinting at its preciousness. The weight of the coin went from 1/70 of a pound (measure established by predecessor Marcus Aurelius Carus) to 1/60 of a pound, totalling 5.45 grams[392]. Then the *argenteus* was introduced, a new silver coin that weighed 3.4 grams and had a precious metal content of about 92 to 95%, a rarity for the time[393]. Finally, the *follis* made its appearance, a silver-plated bronze coin weighing 10.52 grams, which should have played the role of "people's currency" in the wake of the *sestertius* at the height of the imperial era[394]. The system should have responded accordingly to the following changes: 1 *solidus* would have been equivalent to 20 *argentei*, 1 *argenteus* would have been equivalent to 4 *folles*, and 1 *follis* would have been equivalent to 5 *denarii*[395].

This reform, as already mentioned, was accompanied by large investments in the construction (think of the palace in Split, Croatia) and in the military fields. Large defensive valleys were built in these years, not counting the heavy expenses associated with the troops. Diocletian's purpose was very clear: to revive the old bimetallic system, restoring the status of the silver coin that had been lost after the civil wars and compromised by the hyperinflation of the third century[396].

---

[391] Herodian, *History of the Roman Empire Since the Death of Marcus Aurelius*, 7, 3, 3-6.

[392] A. Wassink, "Inflation and Financial Policy under the Roman Empire to the Price Edict of 301 A.D.", *Historia: Zeitschrift für Alte Geschichte*, Franz Steiner Verlag, Bd. 40, H. 4 (1991), p. 486.

[393] Ibidem, p. 487.

[394] Ibidem, p. 486.

[395] Ibidem, p. 487.

[396] Ibidem.

However, the *argenteus* ended up being stored and sometimes even hoarded, and was only used sporadically by the population (several findings have shown these pieces to be in an incredible state of preservation, revealing that they rarely circulated as part of economic transactions).

"It would have really been a functional system if the calculation unit had not been the *denarius*, a currency already subject to considerable inflation when the new initiative was taken. And inflation was a phenomenon that the emperor could never deal with. Gresham's Law gradually forced these coins (*argenteus* and *solidus*) out of circulation. This meant that the *solidus* did not become a coherent part of the monetary system as Diocletian wanted but rather, remained a fluctuating unit, whose value was measured by its gold content. This had long been the reality for the *aureus*, probably from A.D. 190. Inflation first of all threatened the *argenteus*, which shortly after 293 was gradually being accumulated. Whether or not the circulation of the *follis*, with its much lower silver content, was compromised, it is not very clear. However, we can conclude that just after its introduction, Diocletian's coherent monetary system was seriously damaged.[397]"

This first reorganization, datable to the last years of the third century, was evidently a failure and forced the Tetrarchy to again make changes. These were concretized in an edict in 301. The nominal value of the *argenteus* (the antidote to the *solidus* was abandoned because of its fluctuating nature) was increased by 500%. The reason was that prices probably increased during the period between the first and the second reforms at least five times. [398]

To bolster the edict and to prevent prices from rising any more, Diocletian developed the *Edictum De Pretiis Rerum Venalium*, a legislative provision divided into 32 paragraphs that was aimed at stabilizing the prices of about 1000 different goods and 130 types of labour inside the Roman Empire. The preface to the edict clearly outlines its monumental aims, underlining the emperors' universal role and the eternal city's grandeur.

---

[397] Ibidem, p. 488.
[398] Ibidem, p. 489.

"The national honour and the dignity and majesty of Rome demand that the fortune of our State to which, next to the immortal gods, we may, in memory of the wars which we have successfully waged, return thanks for the tranquil and profoundly quiet condition of the world, be also faithfully administered (...) To be sure, if any spirit of self-restraint were holding in check those practices by which the raging and boundless avarice is inflamed, (...) peradventure there would seem to be room left for shutting our eyes and holding our peace, since the united endurance of men's minds would ameliorate this detestable enormity and pitiable condition; (...) it suits us, who are the watchful parents of the whole human race, that justice step in as an arbiter in the case, in order that the long-hoped-for result, which humanity could not achieve by itself, may, by the remedies which our forethought suggests, be contributed toward the general alleviation of all.[399]"

Not even this edict led to lasting results. Considering that inflation continued to dramatically increase prices, the *maxima* introduced by the tetrarchs were circumvented from the moment their value was lowered. For this reason, the practice of payment in kind proliferated. Elsewhere, a sort of black-market *ante litteram* surged, where people sold goods illegally. Looking at the data that has come to us from specific parts of the empire (especially Egypt), scholars have been able to determine that inflation was serious, comparable to that suffered by Western nations in the 1970s and 1980s of the last century[400]. The emperors never fully understood what was causing inflation because they were not traditionally trained in economics and also because they simply had no example from the past that could have acted as a model for them[401]. It still must be recognized though that the short-term measures taken over the course of decades by Roman imperial actors contributed to keeping an economy afloat for centuries, an economy which, it must be remembered, operated intercontinentally.

---

[399] R. Kent, *The Edict of Diocletian Fixing Maximum Prices*, The University of Pennsylvania Law Review, 1920, pp. 41-42.

[400] P.I. Prodromídis, *Another View on an Old Inflation: Environment and Policies in the Roman Empire up to Diocletian's Price Edict*, Centre of Planning and Economic Research, Athens, February 2006, p. 26-27.

[401] A. Wassink, "Inflation and Financial Policy under the Roman Empire to the Price Edict of 301 A.D.", *Historia: Zeitschrift für Alte Geschichte*, Franz Steiner Verlag, Bd. 40, H. 4 (1991), p. 490.

Rationalizing Religion

"...Do not only yourself worship the divine everywhere and in every way in accordance with the traditions of our fathers, but compel all others to honour it. Those who attempt to distort our religion with strange rites you should abhor and punish, not merely for the sake of the gods (since if a man despises these he will not pay honour to any other being), but because such men, by bringing in new divinities in place of the old, persuade many to adopt foreign practices, from which spring up conspiracies, factions, and cabals, which are far from profitable to a monarchy.[402]"

One can certainly detect an oxymoronic juxtaposition in the title of this paragraph; however, the paranormal has played a clear and defined role since the beginning of Rome's history. Let's clarify one thing at once: religion (*religio*) for Romans bore little relation to the personal conception that we have of faith today, which in Latin would be closer to meaning to the verb *credo*[403].

The meaning of *religio* concerned the honours that the *res publica* (which is to say the state and not the individual) paid to the divine. When he came to power, Octavian had several religious buildings celebrating the origins of Rome rebuilt (in 28 B.C. alone he had eighty-two restored[404]). His goal was to make the new empire continuous with the ancient religious traditions of its founders. It is no coincidence that many of the structures built in the capital were associated directly or indirectly with Octavian the person or the military successes achieved during his rule. Lauded by the great scholars of the time as the restoration of the "good old customs", his efforts actually created a powerful new symbol of religiosity. The figure of the *princeps* became an object of worship[405].

---

[402] Cassius Dio, *Roman History*, 52, 36, 1-2: The passage contains advice from Gaius Cilnius Meseus to Octavian on the subject of being inherently attached to religious policy.

[403] R. Schilling, *Rites, Cultes, Dieux de Rome*, Klincksieck, Paris, 1979, p.74; cit. in J. Scheid, *La religione a Roma*, Laterza, Bari, 1983, p. 8.

[404] M. Beard, J. North, S. Price, *Religions of Rome: Volume 1, A History*, Cambridge University Press, Cambridge (UK), p. 196.

[405] Ibidem, pp. 167-168.

"In 7 B.C. Augustus divided Rome into fourteen districts (*regiones*) and 265 wards (*vici*). This reorganization transformed the cults of the wards: from 7 B.C. onwards they became cults of the Lares Augusti and the Genius Augusti. Their traditional celebrations were also changed. To the old festival of the Lares on 1 May was added a new celebration on 1 August, when the magistrates took up office, probably in honour of the Genius Augusti. The significance of these new cults is clear enough in outline, if not in detail. The Lares (usually translated, all too automatically, as 'household gods') were ancient but obscure deities, seen by some ancient writers as the deified spirits of the dead. On this interpretation, the Lares Augusti would be the emperor's ancestors, and the Genius Augusti, the Spirit of Augustus himself. In other words, the public ward cults now consisted of cults that had previously been the private cults of Augustus and his family, located within his own house.[406]"

The new festivities, combined with the construction of new shrines and temples for the celebration of the new imperial cult, allowed Augustus to be present, spiritually and physically, in every corner of the city and of the empire. But it did not end there. Contrary to what had been commonly done in the past, Augustus tied to his person the perpetual power to officiate religious ceremonies. He maintained the title of *pontifex maximus* (a term later borrowed by the Catholic Church for its position of highest authority), the highest Roman religious office[407]. This remained in effect for decades, unaltered, during the Principate.

The Roman authorities subjected new forms of worship introduced in the capital to rigorous control. They were not analysed only by religious authorities, but also by administrative and judicial authorities. Religion was a profoundly political issue.

It is by no mistake that Roman historiography has found comparisons between the worst Roman emperors and the most outlandish foreign cults. The members of the ruling class could not adhere to these *superstitiones* [408] without encountering both social repercussions and legal consequences.

---

[406] Ibidem, pp. 184-185.

[407] Cassius Dio, *Roman History*, 53, 17, 8.

[408] The term *superstitio* in Latin did not mean "not believing in any deity" but instead meant "excessive worship of deities" and therefore represented "incorrect religious conduct". Tacitus and Pliny the Younger referred to the nascent Christianity as such.

In some cases, the emperors even resorted to mass expulsion of those who followed fringe doctrines. In 28 B.C. Augustus banished believers in Egyptian rites from the *pomerium* (the sacred border that delimited the city of Rome) and in 21 B.C. he extended the banishment farther to the outskirts[409]. The Romans held an "ethnic" conception of religion. The empire accepted that every people had its own beliefs, practiced within a limited area. Yet when these beliefs started to circulate more widely in Rome and undermine its own religious traditions, they became threatening and therefore subject to repression by the imperial authorities. The Roman religious system withstood the first two centuries.

However, during the reign of the Severi, the cracks began to show. New cults had managed to insinuate and weave themselves into the Roman social fabric, often helped by influential people of the inner circle of power, or even emperors themselves. Consider, for example, Elagabalus' attempt to replace Jupiter with the solar deity of Asian origin, El-Gabal. Christianity was also growing, especially in the eastern provinces of the empire. Its diffusion, however, did not motivate reactions as brutal as the first persecutions ordered by the emperors Decius and Valerian in the middle of the third century. The followers of Christ had been ignored for decades, while hundreds of other cults coexisted in the Mediterranean from the beginning of Roman rule, with the more or less tacit approval of the imperial authorities.

Religious repression had a systemic reason. During the Principate, the inhabitants of the empire had developed an ever-greater distaste for traditional religion and started to look elsewhere for answers to existential questions[410]. Anything that aggravated the situation in which

---

[409] Cassius Dio, *Roman History*, 53, 2, 4 and 54, 6, 6.

[410] M. Beard, J. North, S. Price, *Religions of Rome: Volume 1, A History*, Cambridge University Press, Cambridge (UK), pp. 289-291, and also J. Neusner, B. Chilton, *Religious Tolerance in World Religions*, Templeton Press, 2008, p. 72. "But it must have seemed to the Roman nobles and ordinary citizens that, if the Roman Jupiter, Juno and Minerva had been tested against the Christian Father, Son and Holy Spirit, the *pax deorum* and the *pax Romana* would be dispelled. The angry gods would surely punish Rome (...). Rapid political dissolution had already signalled religious disaffection with pax *deorum*."

Rome found itself in the third century was met with harsh retaliatory measures. These were taken against foreign cults such as Christianity. Christians began to constitute a growing threat from the political point of view since they were more and more hierarchically organized.

"After having executed their Roman leader Saint Fabian, it seems that Decius said: I would prefer to receive news of a pretender to the throne *rather than of another bishop in Rome.*[411]"

Decius had promulgated an edict that ordered all the inhabitants of the empire to sacrifice to the gods. He specified no obligation to convert nor which deities to honour. What really interested the emperor was protecting a particular rite, sacrifice, which communicated obedience to the Roman authorities[412]. Christians were not the only recipients of this provision[413]. All followers of foreign cults had to prove that they had always made sacrifices with the Roman religion and the emperor in mind. During this anarchical period, the political value of Decius' decision is very clear. Decius, remember, was a promoter of the Latin tradition and campaigned to restore it. The imperial edict should be seen as an attempt to bring the people of the classical world together at a time of serious division and confusion.

Religion as cohesion

An early and radical change in religious politics occurred following the persecution of Valerian. And the driver of this break from the past was once again Gallienus. Following the capture of his father, the

---

[411] M. Grant, *Climax of Rome*, Phoenix, New edition (1997), p. 229.

[412] G.T. Oborn, "Why Did Decius and Valerian Proscribe Christianity?", *Church History*, Vol. 2, Cambridge University Press, Cambridge (UK), No. 2 (Jun., 1933), pp. 68: "Decius understood that, unless forces could be united in such a way as to allow him to fight the threatening dissolution, internal and external, the empire would collapse. (...) All the citizens were called to declare their loyalty. It was a test of patriotism in the same way as religious fervor."

[413] P.F. Esler, *The Early Christian World – Vol.2*, Routledge, 2000, pp. 827–829.

emperor adopted a completely different process in terms of managing religious minorities, Christians in particular. Gallienus wrote to the Egyptian bishops that Christians could resume their activities and restore their places of worship[414].

"The Emperor Caesar, Publius, Licinius, Gallienus, Pius, Felix, Augustus, to Dionysius, Pinnas, Demetrius, and the other bishops. I have ordered the bounty of my gift to be declared through all the world, that they may depart from the places of religious worship. And for this purpose, you may use this copy of my rescript[415], that no one may molest you.[416]"

Thanks to the imperial provision, for the first time in its history, Christianity could enjoy a form of protection by the law. The *superstitio* became *religio*. But why did Gallienus deviate so much from the policies implemented by his predecessors? Christianity was potentially dangerous and it was developing an intimidating organizational structure. Once again it is necessary to take into account the situation into which Gallienus stepped. Gallienus wanted to concentrate completely on the defense of the Danubian border without having to worry about any more riots among the citizenry. Leaving Christians in peace was a measure of political realism especially since many of them now held high-ranking posts in the capital.

Yet there is more. Several scholars have tried to go deeper into the reasons that led Gallienus to take an innovative approach and tolerate Christianity as he did. Some have put forward the hypothesis that he was simply disinterested in the Christian community while others have argued that the proverbial Roman fear of foreigners was the main motivation for the provision. An excellent ruler like Gallienus would leave nothing to chance in an acute crisis situation. That is precisely why we suggest that there were deeper reasons. There is yet another theory, which appears congruent with the portrait of Gallienus that we

---

[414] L. de Blois, *The Policy of the Emperor Gallienus*, E.J. Brill, Leiden, 1997, pp. 178.

[415] The "rescriptum principis" was the imperial response of the emperor to a question asked by individuals or members of the public administration. The response often became a source of law.

[416] Eusebius of Cesarea, *Church History*, 7, 13, 2.

have sketched so far, although it is judged by some to be an exaggeration[417]. After the capture of Valerian in Edessa, the eastern part of the empire fell into chaos. Shapur I's troops ran rampant in Syria; meanwhile, a Roman officer named Macrianus had proclaimed himself emperor. He had been the principal executor of the persecutions of Christians during the last years in Egypt. Gallienus must have had this in mind and must have known that those faithful to Christianity were very numerous in the Mediterranean East. He realized that, by putting an end to the persecutions carried out by his father, he might generate supporters in the fight against the usurper Macrianus. It worked. Pope Dionysius of Alexandria sided with Gallienus against the usurpers[418]. Most of the Christians who had supported Macrianus and his allies defected as soon as they learned of the legal guarantee for their religion assured by the emperor[419]. In Antioch a new bishop was elected, Paul of Samosata, who was very close to the court of Palmyra. It is very likely that Paul pushed the Christian community of Syria to support Odaenathus (and therefore Gallienus) in the fight against the usurper Macrianus[420].

The aims of Gallienus were more extensive than that. The imperial rescript can be further explained by understanding his strategic and military vision. As noted by the historian Lukas de Blois[421], it was not unlikely that Christians could have supported the Persians. Gallienus had well-founded reasons for fearing such an eventuality. During those years in Antioch, a large part of the population had expressed the will to move to the side of the Sassanids, supporting a pro-Persian named

---

[417] C. J. Haas, "Imperial Religious Policy and Valerian's Persecution of the Church, A.D. 257-260", *Church History*, Cambridge University Press, Cambridge (UK), Vol. 52, No. 2 (Jun., 1983), pp. 139.

[418] L. de Blois, "Traditional Virtues and New Spiritual Qualities in Third Century Views of Empire, Emperorship and Practical Politics", *Mnemosyne*, Brill, Fourth Series, Vol. 47, Fasc. 2 (Apr., 1994), p. 175.

[419] S. I. Oost, "The Alexandrian Seditions under Philip and Gallienus", *Classical Philology*, The University of Chicago Press, Vol. 56, No. 1 (Jan., 1961), pp. 15.

[420] L. de Blois, *The Policy of the Emperor Gallienus*, E.J. Brill, Leiden, 1997, pp. 184-185.

[421] Ibidem.

Cyriades[422]. Invading Syria in 253, Shapur had also taken several Christians as prisoners, including the Bishop of Antioch, Demetrian. The latter was treated with respect by the Persians and was even allowed to found a *diocese* at Beth Lapat (in modern-day Iran)[423].

It would have been an easy choice for Syrian Christians to opt for the inclusive government of the Sassanid Empire instead of being persecuted in Rome. Gallienus could not allow a community as important as the Christians to fall into the arms of the empire's main antagonist in the East. At the time, there were too few men to risk antagonizing the enemy and facing their army. The Persians could have taken advantage of this by occupying (and not necessarily striking) locations vital to the Roman defensive strategy like Antioch and Edessa in which the Christian community was numerous and well rooted. As soon as he became the only emperor, Gallienus immediately weakened the *soft power*[424] wielded by Shapur by completely modifying the religious policy promoted by his father.

Certainly, Christianity did not cease to be a threat to Roman power. The emperor had only decided to change the weapons with which to fight the followers of the Nazarene. Typical of Gallienus, a less direct approach prevailed. Persecutions gave way to cultural confrontations[425]. There was a great development in classical culture that sprang forth in the sixties of the third century. It is no coincidence that the emperor

---

[422] E.S. Bouchier, *A Short History of Antioch 300 B.C. - A.D. 1268*, Blackwell, Oxford (UK), 1921, p. 120: "The Empire was at this time so weak and distracted that Shapur was easily induced to attempt an invasion, and encamped a few miles off the city to see if resistance was intended. The more cautious citizens fled, but the majority, with their love of novelty, some, indeed, sympathizing with the idle and luxurious Cyriades, remained, and accepted this worthless Persian vassal as their ruler."

[423] W. Baum, D.W. Winkler, *The Church of the East: A Concise History*, Routledge, London, 2003, p. 9. Beth Lapat (in Persian *Gundeshapur*) was the cultural centre of the Sassanid Empire and home to many prisoners of Greek or Roman origin captured during Persian military operations in the Near East.

[424] The term "soft power" in the context of international relations theory means the ability to attract and persuade through intangible resources of a political, cultural and social nature. This is opposed to "hard power", the use of military force.

[425] L. de Blois, *The Policy of the Emperor Gallienus*, E.J. Brill, Leiden, 1997, pp. 185-186.

had great respect for the philosopher Plotinus and Neoplatonism, which were in opposition to the new Eastern religions. Although his high regard did not translate into concrete support (the Roman government did not grant Plotinus the funds to build a philosophical centre in Campania because it could not afford to invest funds into projects that did not promise a short-term political impact)[426], the ideology of the imperial figure was influenced by the influx of new philosophies.

"Gallienus seems to have adhered to the ideas of Plotinus regarding the figure of the sovereign, rooted in Pythagoreanism, which envisaged a sovereign inspired by the divine that occupied an intermediate position between the Supreme God and the world that he must protect.[427]"

A metamorphosis was underway. On the one hand, the emperor acquired a new form of divine legitimacy and on the other hand, he positioned himself as a figure capable of bringing people closer to the traditional divinity. Had Gallienus perceived what ordinary people saw in Christianity and tried to fulfill that popular need with a presentation that was based on classical culture? Perhaps, although it is impossible to say with any certainty. However, the emperor remained a strong supporter of the Greek-Roman religion, even promoting it by travelling to Athens (in 264), considered by many to be the spiritual capital of classical culture [428]. The imperial mints spewed out coins (a fundamental propaganda tool of the time) that portrayed the "god Gallienus" amongst a select group of gods, referred to as *conservatores*. There were many combinations with the first princeps Augustus in which the emperor seemed to want to identify himself as a bearer of peace and prosperity. There were others with Alexander, the ideal model of the Roman world since the days of the Republic.

---

[426] D. Armstrong, "Gallienus in Athens, 264", *Zeitschrift für Papyrologie und Epigraphik*, Dr. Rudolf Habelt GmbH, Bd. 70 (1987), p. 235.

[427] E. Manders, *Coining Images of Power, Patterns in Representation of Roman Emperor on Imperial Coinage, A.D. 193-284*, Brill, Leiden, 2012, p. 290.

[428] A. Alfoldi, *Studien zur Geschichte der Weltkrise des 3. Jahrhunderts nach Christus*, Wissenschaftliche Buchgesellschaft, Darmstadt, 1967, pp. 16-54/245-263.

Here the aim was also political. It was necessary to strengthen the fragile imperial position, weakened by the shameful capture of Valerian in 260, before all of Roman society, in particular the army.

Among the many divinities invoked by the imperial coinage there was a god who was an outsider to the Olympic pantheon: *Sol Invictus*, an eastern divinity that Elagabalus favoured in the capital during his rule. Why revive a god that had been associated with one of the worst emperors of Rome? The senatorial class already had a poor opinion of Gallienus and it would have been deleterious to further exacerbate relations. The emperor had valid reasons for his choice. *Sol* exerted enormous influence on Roman soldiers. Moreover, belief in *Sol* was diffused in areas that corresponded to those in which the population was feeling the advances of the new imperial and universal spirit of Persia[429]. Gallienus failed to enhance the specific importance of *Sol Invictus*. While he was besieging the usurper Aureolus (his ex *magister equitum*) at Mediolanum, the emperor died. Some point to a conspiracy while others say that he died because of injuries sustained while fighting[430].

Sun worship was officially recognized during the time of the Platonic successor of Gallienus, Aurelian. It must be said that worshipping the sun was not unknown in Rome. It seems that King Titus Tatius had established adoration of the sun[431] in the city at the time of the monarchy. This is not at all surprising. Worship of the sun was present in all ancient religions in various ways. It was exactly what the Roman political actors were looking for. The syncretic potential of the *Sol* supported the world reunification desired by the imperial government.

---

[429] M.P. Canepa, *The Two Eyes of the Earth: Art and Ritual of Kingship between Rome and Sasanian Iran*, University of California Press, Berkeley, 2010, pp. 81-82.

[430] For the conspiracy theory: Historia Augusta, *The Two Gallieni*, 14; for the death in battle theory: Aurelius Victor, *De Caesaribus*, 33, 20-28.

[431] Varro, *De lingua Latina*, 5, 68.

"... during this politically and militarily difficult period, every emperor needed to rely on political and, above all, moral unity in the face of the dangers that threatened him. This unity could be manifested in religion; couldn't a deity crystallize this longed-for unity? Why not choose a divinity whose integration the Roman world had accepted and which, already for many, united all the virtues of the other deities within itself? *Sol* could play that role. In fact, it cannot be forgotten that the Sun was, for many philosophers and rhetoricians, the perfect choice.[432]"

Aurelian's abilities were not limited to the battlefield. The promotion of sun worship happened in conjunction with the surrender of Palmyra. The emperor spoke of having had a vision of the Sun god during the most difficult moment of the final battle with Zenobia, in Emesa[433]. All the imperial mints began to produce coins that depicted *Sol Invictus* as the principal patron of the government of Aurelian, the divinity who gave power in a totally transcendent manner to his chosen one. A temple was built in honour of the god on the slopes of the Quirinal in Rome and a new priestly group was created: the *pontifices solis invicti*. A day of celebration was chosen: December 25. This day was called *Dies Natalis Solis Invicti*, the day of the birth of the Sun (whose popularity would then be exploited by Christianity which determined it to be the day of Jesus' birth).

As the basis for a cult, the choice of *Sol* was undoubtedly made with the military in mind; however, there were other reasons. One was to distance the army from the emperor. As previous chapters have emphasized, political instability in the Roman world in the third century was due in large part to the fact that the legions now provided legitimacy to the pretenders to the throne. It seems that Aurelian wanted to change this pattern by plucking from the sky a source of unchallenged imperial power. This statement might be considered far-fetched but it must be noted that he probably was the first sovereign acclaimed "by the Grace of God". A prelude to what came a few centuries later in Europe.

---

[432] J.P. Martin, "Sol Invictus : Des Sévères à la Tétrarchie d'après les monnaies", *Cahiers du Centre Gustave Glotz*, Editions de Boccard, Vol. 11 (2000), pp. 306-307.

[433] Historia Augusta, *Aurelian*, 25, 3-6.

An antoninianus from the Siscia mint (modern-day Croatia): on the left, Aurelian with a corona radiata, symbolizing the sun's power; on the right, Aurelian shaking hands with the goddess Concordia, representing peace among all the Roman armies and the emperor (CONCORDIA MILITUM).

(© Wikicommons / Rasiel Suarez)

The elevated status of sun worship must not, however, be overstated. The Roman religion continued to be polytheistic, its pre-existing personalities simply coexisting alongside a new protagonist. No restraints had been placed on the traditional celebrations of the Olympic pantheon. Aurelian continued to play the role of guarantor of the major religions of the empire.

For the first time in its history, Christianity submitted to the judgment of the Roman authorities. Paul of Samosata, Bishop of Antioch, was named as being guilty of licentious conduct. He also denied the sanctity of Christ, something that the high Christian authorities could not allow in an important and well-populated bishopric like that of Antioch. When the Mediterranean East was brought back under the dominion of Rome, the Church sent emissaries to the emperor to settle the matter. Aurelian had several reasons to accept this appeal. Firstly, Paul of Samosata had been the protégé of the rebel Zenobia and had many followers in Syria.

Allowing such a character to dominate an area recently brought to order would have been more than inconvenient. Secondly, to depose the heretic bishop would have guaranteed the empire the gratitude and loyalty of the Christian community and its leaders[434]. This was the same wise assessment that probably led Gallienus to stop the persecutions. After all, the Sassanids were a constant threat and their attractiveness could create serious problems. The situation needed to be stabilized. For this reason, Aurelian decided to give an audience to the emissaries. His response was brief and impartial: Antioch would have a bishop designated by Rome. The arbitration revealed a certain continuity with the policy of openness to Christianity. Aurelian had been in Gallienus' entourage for several years and he evidently understood the reasons for the cessation of the persecutions wanted by his predecessor[435]. The rumour that Aurelian wanted to reinstate persecutions is considered groundless. Religious repression, in a newly reunited empire, would have done nothing but increase instability and undermine the territorial victories it had just achieved. Historians who report this news, Eusebius and Lactantius, had every interest in diminishing the image of Aurelian as the emperor "friend to the Christians" while favouring their powerful patron, Constantine[436].

The association between the imperial government and Christianity was violently broken with the advent of the Tetrarchy. A season of religious repression began during this period, known to history as the "Great Persecution". It is said that the event that triggered it took place in Antioch, where Diocletian and Galerius met following the victorious Persian campaign. Here, in the presence of the military and administrative heads of the empire, sacrifices were made in honour of the traditional deities. However, something went wrong: the priests told the emperors that the religious rites were being marred by the presence of "profane" people. It was rumoured that someone had made the sign of the cross.

---

[434] P. Hurley, "Some Thoughts on the Emperor Aurelian as "Persecutor"", *The Classical World*, Vol. 106, The Johns Hopkins University Press, No. 1 (Fall 2012), pp. 80-81.
[435] Ibidem, p. 88.
[436] Ibidem, pp. 83-89.

Diocletian was furious and ordered that everyone in the imperial palace offer sacrifices to the Olympic gods or else be flogged[437]. Christian historians accuse the *Caesar* Galerius especially of having harboured a real fanatical feeling of hatred towards the followers of Christ. A feeling that he incited in his superior Diocletian. But how true is all this? The data shows us that the personal religious fanaticism of the emperor did not form the basis for the decision to persecute Christians.

	Asia Minor	Near East	Danube
Under Diocletian's rule (303-305)	26	31	
Under Galerius' rule (303-305)			14
Under Galerius' rule (not able to be dated)			8
Under Galerius' rule (305-311)	12		12

The number of martyrs recorded in the empire during the Tetrarchy: the first two rows cover the periods in which Diocletian was "Augustus" and Galerius "Caesar"; the last two cover the periods in which Galerius succeeded Diocletian as the "senior partner" of the Tetrarchy.

As can be seen from the table, once he became *Augustus* in the East, Galerius seems to have been responsible for fewer deaths than his colleague[438]. It is interesting to note that, as of 305, he had all the power necessary to unleash his (alleged) anti-Christian wrath on the eastern provinces undisturbed. Evidently, versions of events by Christian historians such as Eusebius and Lactantius lack solid references on this point. There was not an irrational impetus behind

---

[437] Lactantius, *De mortibus persecutorum*, 10.

[438] The table (created on the basis of the *acta martyrum*) and the thesis exonerating Galerius from the responsibility of having instigated the great persecution are taken from: P.S. Davies, "The Origin and Purpose of the Persecution of AD 303", The Journal of Theological Studies, New Series, Vol. 40, Oxford University Press, Oxford (UK), No. 1 (April 1989), pp. 66-94.

the persecutions. Otherwise, Diocletian would not have waited fifteen years for his first anti-Christian ruling (284-299). The emperors considered it inopportune to carry out persecutions with the eastern front in turmoil. The new King of Kings Narseh[439], tolerant of religious minorities, had invaded Syria. Diocletian could not persecute the Church without running the risk of creating pockets of resistance behind the backs of his legionaries. After the losses suffered following the defeat of Galerius in Mesopotamia, the army would not have supported the expulsion of the many Roman soldiers who fought in its ranks. The tetrarchs waited for the war with the Persians to end. Once peace was restored, the Roman government decided to settle accounts with the Christian Church.

The "Great Persecution" was not an effective move. Withholding moral judgments of any kind, which I leave to others, this action lacked both foresight and realism. The idea to celebrate Jupiter Optimus Maximus once again promoted by Diocletian (who not by chance called himself *Iovius*) was anachronistic. There is no doubt that the tetrarchs wanted to gather the population around a shared religious base. But the prevailing mood should have been taken into consideration before initiating harmful, and also expensive, religious persecutions. In a short amount of time, the repression in fact revealed itself to be not only inconclusive, but also counterproductive. The new protagonists on the Roman political scene, Constantine and Maxentius, did not hesitate to challenge it in order to obtain consensus and break the tetrarchic balance[440]. Maxentius allowed the election of a new Pope in Rome, obtaining the support of the Christian community in Italy. When Galerius officially ceased the persecutions in 311 it was too late. Civil war had already flared up and religion became a reason for further division among those who sought power. The political structure devised by Diocletian collapsed inexorably.

---

[439] "Narseh", *iranicaonline.org*, (retrieved November 22, 2018).
[440] T.D. Barnes, *Constantine and Eusebius*, Harvard University Press, Cambridge (MA), 1981, 28-30/38.

By including the new faith and relating it to the many other *licitae* religions, the empire would have diminished the exceptional character of Christianity. In this sense, the policies of Gallienus and Aurelian should have provided a powerful precedent, demonstrating how the empire and church could coexist.

"The forty years or so that divide Gallienus' edict from the beginning of the Diocletian persecution, represent a unique moment in the history of the relationship between state and church: a period of peaceful coexistence not only in fact, but also in law, in which Christianity, as Judaism had long been, was a *religio licita* in an officially pagan state. To the state Christianity offered the loyal collaboration of its faithful, who began to take on without reserve, full citizenship, offices and responsibilities. The empire and the church had a legal relationship that did not tempt the state to interfere with doctrinal issues. This period was also marked by syncretism with sun worship, developing the conditions set forth during the Severian Age. Its aim was to create in the concept of a *summus deus* by many names, the religious unity of a religiously pluralistic empire in which ideological polemic and the struggle of ideas, rejected in the political terrain, were lively parts of free cultural exchange.[441]"

In light of what has been said, the work of Constantine, considered the "Champion of Christianity" appears less impactful. Certainly, his government promoted the new religion like never before. However, his was a move that synchronized with the times, motivated by a realistic reading of the socio-political situation of the empire. Even today the popular version is that Constantine was a figure that ruined "Old Rome", forever severing the bond with a victorious past and the pomp that many admire. The truth is that the empire was transforming and the metamorphosis began well before the advent of Constantine. He did nothing but carry on and develop the policies set in motion by Gallienus and Aurelian.

Outside of his real or presumed adherence to Christianity, the reasoning of Constantinople's founder was political rather than religious. If supporting Christianity could provide a more unified base for the empire, he would have done everything to promote it.

---

[441] M. Sordi, *I cristiani e l'impero romano*, Jaca Book, Milan, 2004, pp. 158-159.

This did not bring about the immediate end of other forms of worship. Constantine never stopped supporting and erecting monuments to other deities[442]. The prolonged presence of *Sol Invictus* in imperial iconography deserves special attention. Even after the decisive Battle of the Milvian Bridge (before which Constantine is said to have had a vision of a cross in the sky) sun worship continued to be encouraged by the government. The historian Eusebius tells us of a military prayer that the soldiers had to say on the "day of the sun" (Sunday). It involved the invocation of a deity that granted victory in battle and ensured the continuation of the lineage of Constantine.

The intent of the imperial government was clear. It was to consolidate the needs of different belief systems present in the empire, allowing Christians and non-Christians to be able to pray together for a single common good: Rome.[443]

---

[442] J. Burckhardt, *Costantino il Grande e i suoi tempi*, Longanesi, Milan, 1957, p. 539. "While he and his mother festooned Palestine and the empire's great cities with lavish churches, he also built pagan temples in the new Constantinople. Two of these, the Temple of the Mother of the Gods and the Temple of the Dioscuri, may have simply been decorative buildings intended to house statues and works of art. By comparison, the Temple of the *Tyche* and its statue personified the city and were presented as a place and object of worship, respectively."

[443] "Costantino e il Sol Invictus", *treccani.it*, (retrieved November 27, 2018).

Coin minted in Pavia depicting Constantine (in the foreground)
alongside Sol Invictus.
For the duration of his rule, the emperor did not stop
endorsing pre-existing deities.

(© Wikicommons / Marie-Lan Nguyen)

Fourth Chapter

Connections with contemporary times

"The challenges we face require *strategic patience and persistence*. They require us to take our responsibilities seriously and make the smart investments in the foundations of our national power. Therefore, I will continue to pursue a comprehensive agenda that draws on all elements of our national strength, that is attuned to the strategic risks and opportunities we face, and that is guided by the principles and priorities set out in this strategy.[444]"

We come to the present day. As has been repeatedly noted in the previous chapters, it is not always the case that empires are in the habit of looking back on history to avoid making the mistakes of the past. Currently, the hegemonic power in the international system is the United States of America. This is a power that has secured global hegemony through economic dominance as well as victories in two world wars. Despite this, according to more than a few observers, the United States ought to be on the decline[445]. Can it be said that American politicians are operating in a similar way to their Roman counterparts in Late Antiquity? Obviously, making direct comparisons between two epochs so far apart is very difficult. Nevertheless, one thing is certain: the problem of managing too many commitments that the Roman Empire faced in the third century is not unlike the current reality of the United States. With this as a starting point, we can better understand how one of the world's superpowers can deal with a situation similar to the one in which Rome found itself 1700 years ago.

---

[444] *US National Security Strategy 2015: Introduction.*
[445] J. Heer, "Are We Witnessing the Fall of the American Empire?", *The New Republic*, March 7, 2018.

The American situation

The total victory achieved at the end of the Second World War revealed to the world the superpower that was the United States. The attack on Pearl Harbor awoke a giant that in a few years proved indomitable to enemies and friends alike. Industrial production, technology and armaments allowed the United States to step into the role of world hegemonic power.

"Since 1945, the United States has gradually expanded the interpretation and extent of its territorial commitments. The Truman and Eisenhower Doctrines, for example, added or attempted to add parts of the northern Mediterranean littoral, Southwest Asia, and the Middle East to early commitments to the defense of Western Europe and Japan. The incorporation of South Korea, once regarded as outside the perimeter, was brought about during the Korean War, just as much of the former French presence in Indochina was gradually assumed by the Americans between 1954 and 1965. Similarly, the former British role in the Indian Ocean and Persian/Arabian Gulf was also absorbed by the United States in the 1970s. Most recently, changes within Nicaragua and El Salvador have restimulated the traditional American presence in the Caribbean and Central America.[446]"

The expansionist push has slowed down since the 1980s. Fear of decline that plagues all hegemonies has been materializing in the rooms of the White House. Moreover, following the fall of the Berlin Wall, new powers began to emerge. Americans have had to think seriously about reorganizing their international commitments if they do not want history to catch them unprepared. The concept of retrenchment has gained recognition only since the Obama administration. The first African American president had to manage circumstances that were nothing short of disastrous; in particular, the economic and financial crisis that erupted in 2008 as well as two bloody wars on the Asian continent (Afghanistan and Iraq).

---

[446] W. R. Thompson, G. Zuk, "World Power and the Strategic Trap of Territorial Commitments", *International Studies Quarterly*, Wiley on behalf of The International Studies Association, Vol. 30, No. 3 (Sep. 1986), p. 265.

These wars were real financial *black holes* for the United States because of the huge military resources that were required. The attack on the Twin Towers in 2001 triggered a rapid surge in American expenditures. In 2012, U.S. defense spending accounted for 52% of all military spending of all other countries on the globe[447]. Since September 11th, more than one million soldiers have been employed in the fight against terrorism, and considerable economic effort has been made.

"As of August 2005, the US Congress had already approved four spending bills for Iraq with funds totalling $204.4 billion and was in the process of approving a "bridge fund" for $45.3 billion to cover operations before another supplemental spending package could be passed in Spring 2006. The IPS made an interesting analysis showing that if the cost of the war as of August 2005 was broken down per person in the United States, the cost at that time would be $727, making the Iraq War the most expensive military effort in the last 60 years. As of July 11, 2007, the cost had more than doubled the August 2005 amount as it stood at over $445 million.[448]"

During his presidency, Obama tried to mitigate the situation, lowering defense spending from 5% of the GDP in 2010 to around 3% at the end of his term. Likewise, the national defense budget went from 722 billion dollars in 2010 to approximately 580 billion in 2015[449]. In terms of territory, the area most affected by the retrenchment was undoubtedly the Middle East. The withdrawal of American troops from Iraq, which was one of Obama's campaign promises during the first election, was finally carried out in 2011[450]. Political disengagement also marked the Syrian conflict. When Bashar Al Assad's government stepped over the so-called "red line" drawn by the American president (the use of toxic gases), the United States preferred not to directly engage the Alawite regime.

---

[447] F. Heisbourg, W. Ischinger, G. Robertson, K. Schake, T. Valasek, *All Alone? What US Retrenchment Means for Europe and NATO*, Centre for European Reform, 2012, p. 6.

[448] S. Lendman, J.J. Asongu, *The Iraq Quagmire: The Price of Imperial Arrogance*, Greenview Pub Co, 2007, pp. 25-26.

[449] M. Wozniak, "The Obama Doctrine – U.S. Strategic Retrenchment and its Consequences", *Securitologia*, No 2/2015, p. 62.

[450] Ibidem, p. 63.

Obama's *modus operandi* created many problems. It has left its main ally in the region, Israel, disgruntled. Moreover, the Iraqi government now finds itself facing new aggressive enemies (ISIS namely)[451]. However, at least the strategy did not see the United States continue to procrastinate while causing more bloodshed. Following the death of Osama Bin Laden, troops are expected to retreat in like manner from Afghanistan.

However, this retreat has been slowed down. Inadequacies within the Afghan government in combination with Russian and Chinese support of Taliban militias[452] have greatly complicated matters. The U.S. government was forced to adopt a "slow withdrawal" and delay the disengagement of its troops. The objective is to make the separation from the Afghan war theater as painless as possible.

Despite these complications, the American presence has decreased from approximately 100,000 troops in 2010 to 9,800 in 2015. A disengagement policy can also be detected in the Euro-Mediterranean sector, where the United States hoped for the fall of Gaddafi while leaving France and England to do the "dirty work[453]". The change in attitude can also be explained by the conduct of European allies. In recent years, countries in the European Union have based 80% of their effective defense on the troops stationed there by the United States. On paper, their transoceanic ally provides 1 million more troops[454].

---

[451] R. Fontaine, "Restraint and Its Discontents", *National Review*, January 23, 2017.

[452] B. Chellaney, "No Easy Escape from Afghan War for Trump", *Nikkei Asian Review*, October 2, 2018: Trump had to increase American presence in Afghanistan with 5,000 marines.

[453] F. Heisbourg, W. Ischinger, G. Robertson, K. Schake, T. Valasek, *All Alone? What US Retrenchment Means for Europe and NATO*, Centre for European Reform, 2012, p. 9.

[454] Ibidem, p. 5.

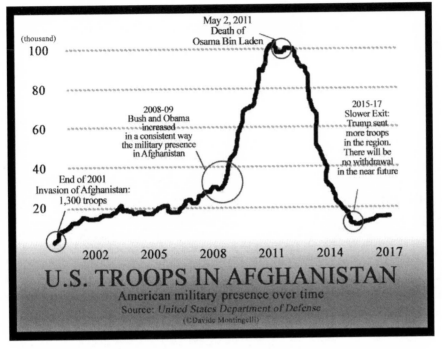

May 2, 2011
Death of
Osama Bin Laden

2008-09
Bush and Obama
increased
in a consistent way
the military presence
in Afghanistan

2015-17
Slower Exit:
Trump sent
more troops
in the region.
There will be
no withdrawal
in the near future

End of 2001
Invasion of Afghanistan:
1,300 troops

2002   2005   2008   2011   2014   2017

U.S. TROOPS IN AFGHANISTAN
American military presence over time
Source: *United States Department of Defense*
(©Davide Montingelli)

U.S. military presence in Afghan territory.
The complete withdrawal of American troops was prevented
by renewed Taliban activity.
President Trump has planned a vigorous deployment of troops
to maintain control of the area.

This is unsustainable for the United States. It is no coincidence that the Americans have planned the withdrawal of large numbers of troops and the closure of various military structures on the old continent[455]. As of 2009, only Greece, France, Albania and Great Britain have allocated the minimum of 2% of GDP for defense purposes established by NATO. The percentage goal is to ensure that European countries take on the political and military responsibility of defending their territories.

---

[455] Ibidem, p. 14.

Cutting down military obligations is highly significant. The crusade launched in defense of democracy against terrorism that began at the beginning of the new millennium has piled commitment after commitment onto the United States. As a result, Americans have lost sight of other potential threats to their pre-eminent status that are on the rise. In this regard, it is the People's Republic of China that creates most concerns.

Let it be made clear, the United States holds undisputed military power and has an extensive reach. China has only one military base outside its borders (in Djibouti, opened in 2016) while the Americans can boast of more than 600 military bases scattered across the globe. Added to those are 11 U.S. aircraft carriers, more than twice those currently owned by Russia, China and India together. At the same time, Xi Jinping's nation, as many observers point out, is experiencing unprecedented growth in every field[456]. China is positioning itself to equal the United States on the international scene. It is no coincidence that Obama reduced American military interference in "peripheral" areas, trying to privilege what will be in the coming decades the main theater: The Far East. With this in mind, the American president has allocated additional units of *marines* in Australia[457].

Donald Trump's arrival in the White House seems to put these prudent makeshift policies in danger. Since he started campaigning, the tycoon has depicted himself as the polar opposite of Obama, the man who will "Make America Great Again" after the ruinous moderation of his predecessor. In 2017's *National Security Strategy* the departure from past policies was striking.

"The United States must reverse recent decisions to reduce the size of the Joint Force and grow the force while modernizing and ensuring readiness.[458]"

---

[456] For a discussion on China's growth: G. Allison, *Destinati alla Guerra. Possono l'America e la Cina sfuggire alla trappola di Tucidide?*, Fazi Editore, Rome, 2018.

[457] "Why US Marines are Deployed to Australia's Far North – Darwinian Evolution", *The Economist*, February 6, 2018.

[458] *US National Security Strategy 2017*, p. 29.

In a short time, Trump has shown that he wishes to abandon his isolationist intentions. Despite the rapprochement with Putin's Russia and great exhortations to European partners to increase military spending, the United States has by no means curtailed their commitments[459]. Indeed, there was a large investment of around $1 billion aimed at "strengthening NATO forces on Europe's borders[460]". It seems that the Atlantic alliance, poorly understood by Trump before the election, will remain active and well-organized, ready to protect all member states, including those that will not reach the minimum of 2% of GDP on military spending[461].

Regarding Afghanistan, the president went back on his electoral promise to totally withdraw and instead gave the green light for sending new troops into this Central Asian furnace[462]. Even in the Far East the approach has been to become more involved rather than disengage. Against the North Korean missile threat, the United States maneuvered in ways not at all aligned with retrenchment. Of course, many observers have been perplexed.

"But we should also tell South Korea that if she desires a nuclear deterrent against an attack by the North, she should build it. Americans should not risk a nuclear war, 8,000 miles away, to defend a South Korea that has 40 times the economy of the North and twice the population.
...No vital U.S. interest requires us, in perpetuity, to be willing to go to war to defend South Korea, especially if that war entails the risk of a nuclear attack on U.S. troops or the American homeland.[463]"

---

[459] P. Dombrowski, S. Reich, "Does Donald Trump Have a Grand Strategy?", *International Affairs* 93: 5 (2017), p. 1027.

[460] G. Jaffe, "National Security Adviser McMaster Defends Trump's Approach with Allies as *Tough Love*", *Washington Post*, June 28, 2017.

[461] P. Dombrowski, S. Reich, "Does Donald Trump Have a Grand Strategy?", *International Affairs* 93: 5 (2017), p. 1027-1028.

[462] J. Beale, "Why are UK and US Sending More Troops to Afghanistan?", *BBC News*, August 13, 2018.

[463] P. J. Buchanan, "An America First Korea policy", *CNS News*, June 30, 2017.

Trump seems to employ an unmistakeable "primacist strategy[464]", in line with that of his more interventionist predecessors. At least it appears as such.

But there is another reality, much deeper and more complex. There are multiple reasons for renewing American military obligations around the world. One of the problems of retrenchment is the danger of abandoning allies that are too weak and, above all else, appearing vulnerable to stronger enemies. In Afghanistan the withdrawal of troops ordered by Obama in 2014 resulted in a sharp deterioration in the military capacity of the Kabul government. As previously mentioned, the interference of Chinese and Russians in favour of the Taliban has been a factor. The vacuum had to be filled quickly. A prolonged lack of troops would have caused serious damage to the American position in Central Asia. Farther east, Trump's policy towards Kim Jong-un appeared initially very aggressive and risky. What seemed like a relationship based on mutual hatred, however, has transformed over time into "tough love". The rapprochement between North Korea and the United States has had a diplomatic result that is anything but insignificant. The American have snatched a very useful potential ally for the future from China's clutches[465]. As for partners in Europe, the United States turned out to be willing to continue to provide military coverage but they have made it known several times that it will not last forever. Many countries from the Old Continent are beginning to rethink their strategies; notably, Great Britain[466].

It can therefore be said that, looking beyond the slogans and clashing personalities of these two politicians, Obama and Trump have pursued the same fundamental strategic plan, according to which the United States aims at optimizing its efforts given the new adversaries operating in the international system[467].

---

[464] P. Dombrowski, S. Reich, "Does Donald Trump Have a Grand Strategy?", *International Affairs* 93: 5 (2017), p. 1022.

[465] B. Chellaney, "Trump's Grand Strategy", *The Japan Times*, August 1, 2018.

[466] E. Baldato, M. Dian, "Trump's Grand Strategy and the Post-American World Order", *Interdisciplinary Political Studies*, Vol. 4, No. 1 (2018), p. 30.

[467] R. Douthat, "The Obama-Trump Grand Strategy", *The New York Times*, June 12,

The tycoon is doing far more than any of his predecessors in recognizing this new reality. The "End of History" as it was conceived of by Francis Fukuyama at the culmination of the twentieth century, which saw the victory of liberal democratic order and the end of the Soviet Union, is now further away than ever. Trump is demonstrating, through both his words and actions, that the United States will find itself in competition with other powers in this century. Chinese growth will likely be the biggest challenge that America will have to confront in the coming years. Its growth does not only concern the economy. Beijing is poised to dramatically alter the political balance in the Far East. For the time being, only harsh statements and sanctions have come from Washington as punishment for Chinese economic subterfuge, but nothing more. The United States must better target its efforts if they want to send a serious response to what will be the main challenger to their hegemony.

Comparisons with the past

It seems that the United States has taken the right path to optimize their position in the world. That path, however, is full of obstacles. It is not enough for many American political actors (though not all) to agree that a policy of retrenchment must be implemented. There are numerous complexities and pitfalls to the real-world application of such a policy. Obama and Trump have taken significant steps towards reducing American engagements abroad but the international system takes time to adjust. All over the globe the United States finds itself forced into a strategic check, unable to proceed with rapid disengagement. What should the country do then? At this point, it would be useful to make a cautious comparison with certain events from the past that share similarities with the current situation; namely, the Habsburg Empire in the seventeenth century and the focus of our analysis, the Roman empire in the third century.

2018.

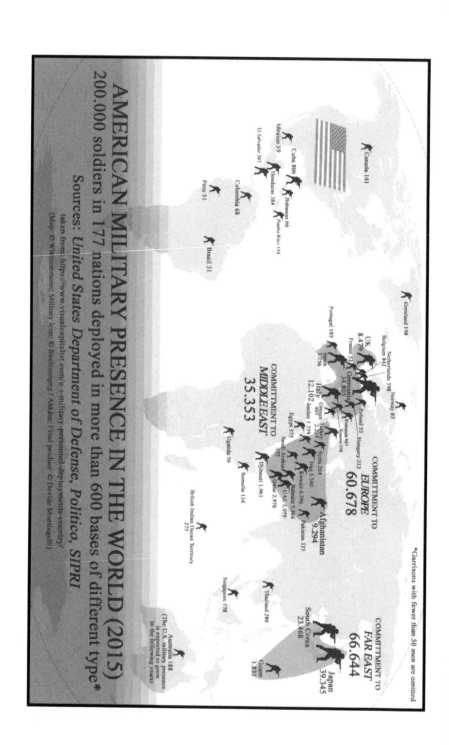

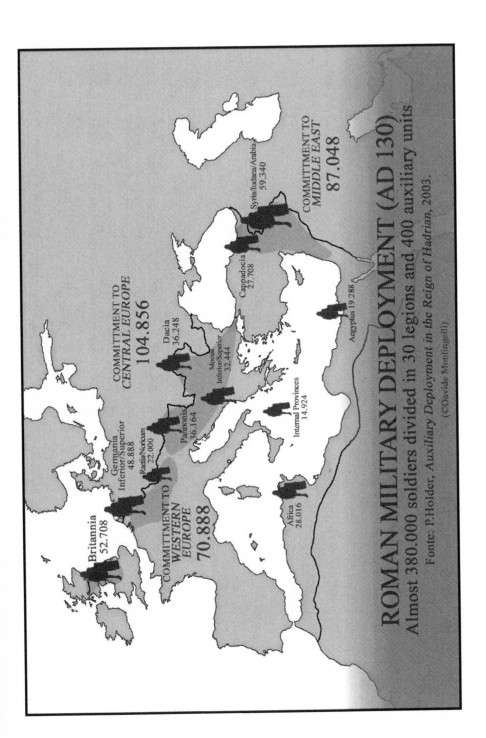

ROMAN MILITARY DEPLOYMENT (AD 130)

Almost 380.000 soldiers divided in 30 legions and 400 auxiliary units

Fonte: P.Holder, *Auxiliary Deployment in the Reign of Hadrian, 2003.*

(©Davide Montingelli)

Britannia
52.708

COMMITMENT TO
WESTERN EUROPE
70.888

Germania
Inferior/Superior
48.888

Raetia/Noricum
22.000

COMMITMENT TO
CENTRAL EUROPE
104.856

Dacia
36.248

Pannonia
36.164

Moesia
Inferior/Superior
32.444

Internal Provinces
14.924

Africa
28.016

Aegyptus 19.288

Cappadocia
27.708

Syria/Iudaea/Arabia
59.340

COMMITTMENT TO
MIDDLE EAST
87.048

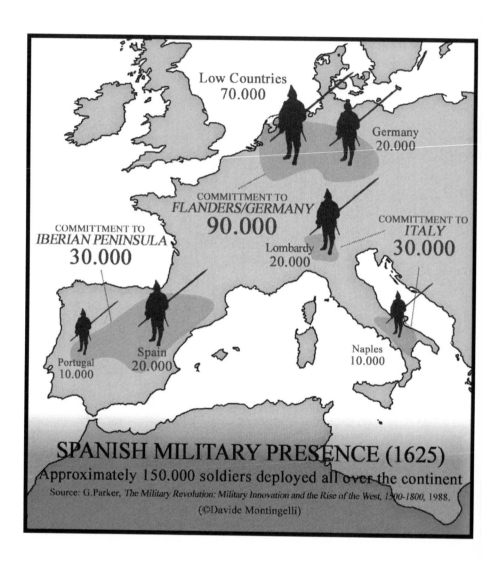

Low Countries
70.000

Germany
20.000

COMMITTMENT TO
FLANDERS/GERMANY
90.000

COMMITTMENT TO
IBERIAN PENINSULA
30.000

COMMITTMENT TO
ITALY
30.000

Lombardy
20.000

Portugal
10.000

Spain
20.000

Naples
10.000

SPANISH MILITARY PRESENCE (1625)
Approximately 150.000 soldiers deployed all over the continent
Source: G.Parker, *The Military Revolution: Military Innovation and the Rise of the West, 1500-1800*, 1988.
(©Davide Montingelli)

The preceding tables represent military deployment of the three hegemonic-imperial entities being examined. Although all three differ in various political aspects, all of them have found themselves at some point in history having to decide whether to withdraw or maintain an extensive presence, keeping their prestige intact but meanwhile accumulating increasingly burdensome costs. For each of these nations, such a commitment seems to present certain strategic difficulties.

	Number of troops by year			
Romans in Dacia	150.000 (106)	36.248 (130)	50.000 (200)	0 (271)
Habsburg in the Low Countries	86.235 (1574)	49.765 (1607)	77.000 (1639)	109.000 (1640)
U.S. in Afghanistan	26.000 (2007)	100.000 (2011)	9.800 (2015)	14.000 (2017)

Number of troops employed by the three hegemonic-imperial entities in the most problematic commitments within their domain.

(© Davide Montingelli)

We have already analysed the first case. Conquered by an imposing military force under the emperor Trajan, Dacia divided powerful tribes like the Iazyges, Gepids and Goths. Its strategic role as a pivot point required the presence of a very large military garrison. During the Crisis of the Third Century, the Roman rulers understood that this province was no longer economically sustainable for the empire's forces. Gallienus and Aurelian set in motion a gradual withdrawal from the area that stretched over more than ten years. The process was far from painless. Even though a good part of the province's population was evacuated on either side of the *limes*, many Roman colonies were devastated by the barbarians. All of the most dangerous tribes in the area swiftly approached the Danube, putting palpable pressure on the provinces of Moesia Inferior and Superior. The makeshift policy also affected domestic politics. In the following years, Roman observers did not fail to condemn the government, specifically the person of Gallienus, for this dishonourable retreat[468]. Fortunately, the manoeuvre worked. Rome had gained the forces withdrawn from Dacia (including two legions) and managed to withstand the barbarian attacks. Retrenchment had made it possible to streamline Roman defense in central and southern Europe. The Lower Danube was a natural barrier which allowed for a smaller deployment of troops than that required by the artificial defense present in Dacia. It was more than just breathing room for the empire. The stability achieved in the sector allowed the Roman troops to go on the offensive. Under Constantine the legions occupied parts of Oltenia and Wallachia, and kept them for at least thirty years[469][470].

Let us now analyze the case of the Habsburg Empire. This empire, unlike the Roman Empire, possessed a dominion made up of non-contiguous territories, which was therefore more difficult to manage. As already mentioned in the first chapter, the commitment that overextended the Habsburg Empire was undoubtedly that of the Netherlands. Overwhelmed by taxes imposed by the Spanish, the Dutch rebelled in 1568 and a bloody eighty-year war began. King Philip II set up an *ad hoc* expeditionary force, called the "Army of Flanders", to bring the rebels under his control. The difficulty of the terrain and the Dutch resistance turned the revolt into a long conflict of attrition.

---

[468] P. Southern, *The Roman Empire from Severus to Constantine* (2001), Routledge, London, 2015, p. 176.

[469] P. Southern, *The Roman Empire from Severus to Constantine* (2001), Routledge, London, 2015, p. Bd., Franz Steiner Verlag, H. 3 (1956), pp. 372-381.

[470] For the table's data, Rome: Y. Le Bohec, *L'esercito romano di Augusto alla fine del III secolo*, Rome, 2008, pp.34/45; P.L. MacKendrick, *The Dacian Stones Speak*, The University of North Carolina Press, 2000, p. 107; I.A. Oltean, *Dacia: Landscape, Colonization and Romanization*, Routledge, 2007, p. 56. Habsburg: G. Parker, *El ejército de Flandes y el Camino Español 1567-1659*, p. 315. USA: R. Check, "Afghanistan war: Trump's Allies and Troop Numbers", *BBC News*, August 22, 2017.

Transport was dangerous so sending troops to the Netherlands was a further *malus* for military operations. Unable to take Atlantic routes, the imperial reinforcements sailed from Barcelona to Liguria and then proceeded on foot to Brussels passing through Lombardy, Switzerland, Franche-Comté, Lorraine and Luxembourg. Approximately 1,000 kilometres long[471], the journey was perilous and troops were vulnerable to enemy ambushes. The war turned out to be a significant drain on Spain's resources.

"Even at the height of the Thirty Years War, five or six times as much money was allocated to the Flanders garrison as to forces in Germany. 'The War in the Netherlands,' observed one Spanish councillor, 'has been the total ruin of this monarchy'. In fact, between 1566 and 1654 Spain sent at least 218 million ducats to the Military Treasury in the Netherlands, considerably more than the sum total (121 million ducats) of the crown's receipts from the Indies (during the same period).[472]"

The benefits of a possible victory would never remotely equal the costs faced to support the *Ejército de Flandes*. If the Habsburgs had succeeded in stifling the rebellion, Dutch rule would not have guaranteed the region's defense since it remained exposed to land invasions from France and maritime raids from England. Why did the Spanish imperial actors stubbornly want to fight such a war? The answer is quite simple: reputation. The rise of Spanish power began with the capture of Granada and the expulsion of the infidels from Iberian lands in 1492. In the years that ensued, the nation defined itself as universal champion of the Catholic faith.

The American Indians, Ottoman Turks and followers of Luther were all equally strangers and enemies within the global order. The Spanish crown oversaw this order and required that they convert or be wiped out. There was no middle ground. Habsburg persistence in Flanders was due to ideology. The Spanish kings neglected to take into consideration that the Dutch theater alone required a more numerous garrison than all their other garrisons of Europe put together.

---

[471] This refers to the journey from Milan to Flanders.
[472] P. Kennedy, *The Rise and Fall of Great Powers*, Unwin Hyman Limited, London, 1988. 50.

Philip II and his successors could not allow Protestantism to proliferate in Europe. It was an affront to their supranational role as a world-ordering power. In Madrid, the thinking was that retreat would embolden and engender enemies of Catholicism in the Pyrenees. So the imperial troops remained in the Netherlands, embroiled in a seemingly never-ending war, which only ended when the crown treasury was exhausted. When most of the expeditionary force had withdrawn from Flanders, Spain was a defeated nation, on the political decline and in the midst of a terrible economic crisis.

The United States seems to have understood what Spanish imperial actors ignored for decades. However, there are some obvious similarities with Spain's failure. For example, the American nation has a universal role similar to the one by which Spain had defined itself since 1492. After the Second World War, the United States stood as a defender of democracy and freedom in the world, often launching "humanitarian attacks" against countries that ran roughshod over these ideals. Although Trump seems to have tempered the ideological role that America has played in past decades, by recognizing the legitimacy of even non-democratic powers[473], moral battles remain an American priority. The crusade against Islamic terrorism remains essential; the current administration calls it a battle of "civilization" (an expression that harkens back to Bush's disastrous doctrines)[474]. It is precisely this line of action that has trapped the United States in what is, for now, the longest running war in their history: the conflict in Afghanistan.

Following the terrorist attack of September 11th, 2001, the invasion was part of the "War on Terror" compelled by the Bush administration. The American troops were tasked with flushing out the instigator of the terrorist attack on the United States, Osama Bin Laden, as well as punishing those who protected him, namely the Taliban government. Over the years, the allied contingent far exceeded 100,000 units. In 2011, Osama Bin Laden was finally found but the country's problems were far from over.

---

[473] E. Baldato, M. Dian, "Trump's Grand Strategy and the Post-American World Order", *Interdisciplinary Political Studies*, Vol. 4, No. 1 (2018), p. 23.

[474] Ibidem, p. 26.

After Obama's first failed attempt at a total withdrawal of troops in 2014, Trump had to replenish the U.S. garrison in light of the threat that the Taliban posed to the new central government. In addition to increasing their military presence, the new administration has revamped its training plan for Afghan forces. It has also decided to put greater diplomatic pressure on Pakistan (to ensure that it does not support the Taliban) and strengthen their partnership with India in order to remove other powers from the area (above all China)[475]. None of these initiatives, however, seems likely to bring the conflict to a conclusion after seventeen years. The numbers are disheartening: operations in Afghanistan have cost approximately $1.07 trillion and in 2015 alone the government put about $60 billion towards the conflict[476]. 2,350 American soldiers have lost their lives and more than 20,000 have been injured. In addition, more than 300,000 have been psychologically traumatized, necessitating long-term medical care projected to cost about $1 trillion over the next forty years[477]. To make matters worse, there have been losses among civilians. Losses for 2017 were estimated to be 10,000 dead and it is expected that there will be even more in 2018[478]. Despite the expenditure of blood and money, the Taliban do not seem to have been weakened at all. They hold more territories than they ever have in fact since the fall of their regime in 2001[479].

The commitment in Afghanistan has become a strategic trap that risks making the United States unprepared for the "Big Game" of the 21st century. As anticipated, the war is not providing rapid results and the other powers are not paying it any heed. Russia is taking small but decisive steps every year to regain its former role as a global power while

---

[475] P. Dombrowski, S. Reich, "Beyond the Tweets: President Trump's Continuity in Military Operations", *Strategic Studies Quarterly*, Vol. 12, Air University Press, No. 2 (SUMMER 2018), pp. 67-69.

[476] K. Amadeo, "Afghanistan War Cost, Timeline and Economic Impact", *The Balance*, August 29, 2018.

[477] Ibidem.

[478] "Why Afghanistan is More Dangerous Than Ever", *BBC News*, September 14, 2018.

[479] M. Pennington, "Pentagon Says War in Afghanistan Costs Taxpayers $45 Billion Per Year", *PBS*, February 6, 2018.

China, according to many observers, is going to overtake the United States by every economic and military standard in a few decades[480]

The situation is not critical and the United States still has much room to maneuver. Washington is the political centre of the world, but China's *soft power* is growing exponentially. The American lifestyle continues to be the undisputed model for millions of people around the globe; the *Stars and Strips* flag still flaps in the wind on every continent. U.S. leaders must "simply" make the decision to put aside their attachment to *grandeur* and reduce the number of obligations in a way that is seen as sensible and gradual by their society and allies. If they were willing to do that than they would avoid the formation of anti-hegemonic coalitions. A diplomatic detente would also be helpful and allay the danger of "imperial overexpansion". The historical cases that we have analyzed are emblematic and consistently demonstrate this point. There is little doubt as to which choice should be made to achieve success. If any American politician happens to read this analysis, he or she would also be wise to consider the famous saying by Cicero: *Historia magistrae vitae*[481].

---

[480] P. MacDonald and J.M. Parent, "Graceful Decline? The Surprising Success of Great Power Retrenchment", *International Security*, Vol. 35, No. 4 (Spring 2011).
[481] Cicero, *De Oratore*, 2, 9, 36.

Conclusion

For those who make empires the subject of their studies, it can be said that the third century is a period with ample teachings and lessons with relevance to the present day. The eternal city, Rome, the capital of the civilized world, was on the verge of collapse. Rome was facing considerable external and internal threats. Fresh barbarian attacks from the outside and infighting among ambitious leaders inside the capital were causing it to crumble.

The empire was staring down the bogeyman of all sovereign entities: division. Palmyra and Gaul had compromised Roman unity; anarchy and violence reared their ugly heads again in territories that had enjoyed centuries of prosperity and tranquillity. Total collapse was more than a creeping fear for the Romans[482]. Traditional attempts to reverse the trend were failing, dragging those who upheld them into the abyss. There was most likely an awareness that something had to change but a succession of emperors, either due to lack of time or courage, simply trudged along, as the empire of Augustus slowly faded. It seemed to be the end for all of the ancient world.

It was at this point that Gallienus came forward. To modern eyes, looking back through centuries of historiography, he was a statesman. It is possible to see in him, as it is in Aurelian and Diocletian, a noble characteristic: humility. These three emperors understood that in order to pull Rome out of the quagmire in which it floundered, profound changes were needed, changes to Roman ways and customs that had been for centuries its strength.

---

[482] G. Alfoldy, "The Crisis of the Third Century as Seen by Contemporaries", *Greek, Roman and Byzantine Studies*, Vol. 15, 1974, pp. 95-96.

In a world where the ruling classes were taught to value honour and greatness, they understood that at this time it was necessary to pull back and radically change their way of waging war.

Gallienus was the initiator of the "Resurgence of Rome". Here was a man, let us remember, who put the needs of the state ahead of his personal desire to avenge the death of his son as well as ahead of his own legacy. As the empire's only ruler, he recognized that the aristocratic class of the Italian peninsula was by now incapable of confronting the crisis. With great courage he decided to open the doors of power to others, individuals of humble origins, mainly from the Balkans, who desired to prove themselves worthy of the responsibility.

"Illyria was the Prussia of the Roman Empire. The Illyrian populations cultivated a long military tradition. Moreover, they had developed a profound deference towards Rome, both as a civilization and a myth. They had assimilated the idea of Rome into their own culture and considered themselves its proud guardians. The Roman Empire was saved by these peasant soldiers. Illyria exemplified Rome's ability to arouse the Roman character in defeated populations. Romanized Illyricum produced not only good soldiers, but also excellent generals.[483]"

The healthy integration cultivated for a long time by the empire was bearing fruit. What Rome gave to Illyria, Illyria returned to Rome at its most desperate moment in its history. The recovery process lasted decades and was arduous, yet in the end produced positive effects. Thankfully, the withdrawal from commitments did not overly encourage opponents; on the contrary, it allowed the entire Roman war machine to be updated. Society was regenerated through an old form of worship made new again: the Sun. The only measures that did not produce the desired results were those of an economic or monetary nature. However, there were numerous mitigating factors. Above all, the imperial actors did not have any knowledge in the field and they were lacking in historical examples that could have given them guidance. In spite of everything, the choices made during this period served, if not to completely staunch, at least to slow down the copious haemorrhaging caused by inflation.

---

[483] G. Ruffolo, *Quando l'Italia era una superpotenza*, Einaudi, 2004, p. 98.

But what would have happened if Rome had fallen?

The empire probably would have fragmented in such a way that everything would have been lost. We will never know.

What is certain is that the steps taken by Gallienus, Aurelian and Diocletian avoided a disaster of this magnitude. Collapse was delayed for two hundred years. In the meantime, Rome had the time to "train" its heirs. In the western part of the empire, the barbarians founded kingdoms steeped in Latin culture. Meanwhile, on the other side of the Mediterranean, the Roman world remained preserved for another millennium in the empire's womb to the East, destined to mark another important page in history. Without the reorganization undertaken in the third century, Constantinople could never have existed. We would not have had Justinian's *Renovatio Imperii* or the dazzling Persian campaign of Heraclius or the splendid Byzantine culture, to which the European Renaissance owes a great debt. This is yet another reason why the third century is a crucial moment in our past.

I will conclude with an idea that permeates this chapter of history: survival requires adaptation. And the Romans did adapt, questioning what they held to be fundamental to their culture. They put past glories aside and looked inward to find the will and humility that have always distinguished them. This was how the greatest empire in history was rescued, once again proving to be a reality in which *one cannot distinguish what separates the possible from the impossible.*[484].

---

[484] S. Mazzarino, *La fine del mondo antico* (1959), Bollati Boringhieri, 2016, pp. 193.

Acknowledgements

To Professor Colombo, for having given me green light to explore such a heterodox theme. I want to also thank Mattia for the patience and dedication in the creation of the cover. Likewise, my gratitude goes to Kirsten (the translator), Maria (the proofreader) and also Mariaida, Costantino, Cristina and Stefano for having contributed in various ways to my writing.
Finally, a special thanks goes to all those who are part of my organization "Renovatio Imperii". You have given me constant and daily encouragement in the writing of this work.

Bibliography

- Agazia Scolastico, *Sul regno di Giustiniano*.
- Alfoldi, A., *Studien zur Geschichte der Weltkrise des 3. Jahrhunderts nach Christus*, Wissenschaftliche Buchgesellschaft, Darmstadt, 1967.
- Alfoldy, G., "The Crisis of the Third Century as Seen by Contemporaries", *Greek, Roman and Byzantine Studies*, Vol. 15, 1974.
- Allison, G., *Destinati alla Guerra. Possono l'America e la Cina sfuggire alla trappola di Tucidide?*, Fazi Editore, Rome, 2018.
- Amadeo, K., "Afghanistan War Cost, Timeline and Economic Impact", *The Balance*, August 29, 2018.
- Ammianus Marcellinus, *Histories*.
- Appian, *The Civil Wars*.
- Armstrong, C.K., *Tyranny of the Weak: North Korea and the World, 1950-1992*, (2013).
- Armstrong, D., "Gallienus in Athens, 264", *Zeitschrift für Papyrologie und Epigraphik*, Dr. Rudolf Habelt GmbH, Bd. 70 (1987).
- Augustus, *Res Gestae Divi Augusti*.
- Aulus Gellius, *Attic Nights*.
- Aurelius Victor, *De Caesaribus*.
- Baldato E., Dian, M., "Trump's Grand Strategy and the Post-American World Order", *Interdisciplinary Political Studies*, Vol. 4, No 1 (2018).
- Balot, R., "Polybius' Advice to the Imperial Republic", *Political Theory*, Sage Publications, Inc. Vol. 38, No. 4 (August 2010), p.
- Barnes, T.D., *Constantine and Eusebius*, Harvard University Press, Cambridge (MA), 1981.

- Baum, W., Winkler, D.W., *The Church of the East: A Concise History*, Routledge, London, 2003.
- Beale, J., "Why are UK and US Sending More Troops to Afghanistan?", BBC News, August 13, 2018.
- Beard, M., J. North, S. Price, *Religions of Rome: Volume 1, A History*, Cambridge University Press, Cambridge (UK), 1998.
- Bernardi, A., *The Economic Problems of the Roman Empire at the Time of Its Decline*, Pontificia Universitas Lateranensis, Rome, 1965.
- de Blois, L., "Traditional Virtues and New Spiritual Qualities in Third Century Views of Empire, Emperorship and Practical Politics", Mnemosyne, Brill, Fourth Series, Vol. 47, Fasc. 2 (Apr., 1994).
- de Blois, L., *The Policy of the Emperor Gallienus*, E.J. Brill, Leiden, 1997.
- de Blois, L., *The Reign of Emperor Philp the Arabian*, Free University, Amsterdam, 1978.
- Brink, C.O., Walbank, F.W., "The Construction of the Sixth Book of Polybius", *The Classical Quarterly*, Cambridge University Press, Cambridge (UK), Vol. 4, No. 3/4 (Jul. - Oct., 1954).
- Boozer, A.L., "Frontiers and Borderlands in Imperial Perspectives: Exploring Rome's Egyptian Frontier", *American Journal of Archaeology*, Archaeological Institute of America, Vol. 117, No. 2 (April 2013).
- Bouchier, E.S., *A Short History of Antioch 300 B.C. - A.D. 1268*, Blackwell, Oxford (UK), 1921.
- Buchanan, P. J., "An America First Korea policy", *CNS News*, June 30, 2017.
- Burckhardt, J., *Costantino il Grande e i suoi tempi*, Longanesi, Milan, 1957.
- Butcher, K., *Debasement and the Decline of Rome* in R. Bland, D. Calomino, *Studies in Ancient Coinage in Honour of Andrew Burnett*, Spink & Son Ltd, London, 2015.
- Caliri, E., "Il Pianto di Scipione Emiliano", *Ricerche di storia an-*

tica, n.s. 5-2013.

- Campbell, B., *The Roman Army, 31 BC – AD 337: A Sourcebook* (1994), Routledge, London, 2006.
- Canepa, M.P., *The Two Eyes of the Earth: Art and Ritual of Kingship between Rome and Sasanian Iran*, University of California Press, Berkeley, 2010.
- Carlà, F., "Tu tantum praefecti mihi studium et annonam in necessariis locis praebe: prefettura al pretorio e annona militaris nel III secolo d. C.", *Historia: Zeitschrift für Alte Geschichte*, Franz Steiner Verlag, Bd. 56, H. 1 (2007).
- Cascarino, G., Sansilvestri, C., *L'esercito romano, Armamento e organizzazione, Vol. III – Dal III secolo alla fine dell'Impero d'Occidente*, Il Cerchio, Rimini, 2009.
- Cassius Dio, *Roman History*.
- Cecconi, G.A., *Da Diocleziano a Costantino: le nuove forme del potere*.
- R. Check, "Afghanistan War: Trump's Allies and Troop Numbers", *BBC News*, August 22, 2017.
- Chellaney, B., "No Easy Escape from Afghan War for Trump", Nikkei Asian Review, October 2, 2018.
- Chellaney, B., "Trump's Grand Strategy", *The Japan Times*, August 1, 2018.
- Cicero, *De Oratore*.
- "Costantino e il Sol Invictus", *treccani.it*, (retrieved November 27, 2018).
- Coulston, J. C. N., "How to Arm a Roman Soldier", *Bulletin of the Institute of Classical Studies. Supplement*, Wiley, No. 71, (1998).
- Cowan, R., *Roman Legionary 58 BC - 69 AD*, Osprey Publishing, 2003.
- Darwin, J.D., "The Fear of Falling: British Politics and Imperial Decline Since 1900", *Transactions of the Royal Historical Society*, Cambridge University Press, Cambridge (UK), Vol.. 36 (1986).
- Davies, M. Jo, "Polybius on the Roman Republic: Foretelling a Fall," *Saber and Scroll*, 2015, Vol. 4: Iss. 2, Article 9.

- Davies, P.S., "The Origin and Purpose of the Persecution of AD 303", *The Journal of Theological Studies*, New Series, Vol. 40, Oxford University Press, Oxford (UK), No. 1 (April 1989).
- Davies, R.W., "The Roman Military Diet", *Britannia*, Vol. 2 (1971).
- Debevoise, N.C., *Political History of Parthia*, University of Chicago Press, 1938.
- Department of Defense, *Sustaining US Global Leadership: Priorities for 21st Century Defense*, (January 2012), 3-4.
- Dexippus, *Scythica*.
- Diegi, R., "Le monete di Aureliano", *Panorama numismatico*, n° 251/May 2010.
- Dixon, K.R., Southermn, P., *Late Roman Army*, 1996.
- Dodgeon M.H., Lieu, S.N.C., *The Roman Eastern Frontier and the Persian Wars (AD 226-363)*.
- Douthat, R., "The Obama-Trump Grand Strategy", *The New York Times*, June 12, 2018.
- Dombrowski, P., Reich, S., "Beyond the Tweets: President Trump's Continuity in Military Operations", *Strategic Studies Quarterly*, Vol. 12, Air University Press, No. 2 (SUMMER 2018).
- Dombrowski, P., S. Reich, "Does Donald Trump Have a Grand Strategy?", *International Affairs* 93: 5 (2017).
- Eadie, J.W., "The Development of Roman Mailed Cavalry", *The Journal of Roman Studies*, Vol. 57, No. 1-2. (1967).
- Eckstein, A.M., "Thucydides, the Outbreak of the Peloponnesian War, and the Foundation of International Systems Theory", *The International History Review*, Vol. 25, No. 4 (Dec. 2003).
- Erdkamp, P., *A Companion to the Roman Army*, Blackwell Publishing, 2007.
- Herodian, *History of the Roman Empire Since the Death of Marcus Aurelius*.
- Esler, P. F., *The Early Christian World – Vol.2*, Routledge, 2000.
- Eusebius of Cesarea, *Church History*.
- Eutropius, *Breviarium ab Urbe condita*.

- E.E. Mills, *The Decline and Fall of British Empire*, Bocardo Press (1905), London.
- Ferrill, A., "Roman Imperial Grand Strategy", *Pubblication of the Association of Ancient Historians 3*, University Press of America, 1991.
- Fontaine, R., "Restraint and Its Discontents", National Review, January 23, 2017.
- Franciosi, G., *Corso storico istituzionale di diritto romano*, Giappichelli, February 2015.
- Frank, R.I., "Ammianus on Roman Taxation", *The American Journal of Philology*, The Johns Hopkins University Press Vol. 93, No. 1, Studies in Honor of Henry T. Rowell (Jan., 1972).
- Frank, T., *An Economic History of Rome* (1927) Batoche Books Limited, 2004.
- "Frontiers of the Roman Empire", *whc.unesco.org*, (retrieved February 15, 2018).
- Gall, L., *Bismarck: The White Revolutionary:1815-1871*.
- Gibbon, E., *The History of the Decline and Fall of the Roman Empire*.
- Gilliam, J.F., "The plague under Marcus Aurelius", *Am. J. Philolog.* 327, 1961.
- Gilpin, R., *War and Change in International Politics*, Cambridge University Press, Cambridge (UK), 1981.
- Jordanes, *De origine actibusque Getarum*.
- Emperor Julian, *Letter to the Athenians*.
- Goldsworthy, A., *The Complete Roman Army*, Thames and Hudson, 2003.
- Goldsworthy, A., *How Rome Fell*, Yale University Press, 2009.
- Goodchild R.G., Ward Perkins, J.B., "The Limes Tripolitanus in the Light of Recent Discoveries", *The Journal of Roman Studies*, Society for the Promotion of Roman Studies, Vol. 39, Parts 1 and 2 (1949).
- Grant, M., *Climax of Rome*, Phoenix, New edition (1997).
- Gudea, N., "The Difensive System of Roman Dacia", *Britannia*,

Society for the Promotion of Roman Studies, Vol. 10 (1979).

- Haas, C. J., "Imperial Religious Policy and Valerian's Persecution of the Church, A.D. 257-260", *Church History*, Cambridge University Press, Cambridge (UK), Vol. 52, No. 2 (Jun., 1983).
- Hartley, A., "O! What a Fall was There: Reflections on the Decline of Britain", *The National Interest*, Center for the National Interest, No. 35 (Spring 1994).
- Heer, J., "Are We Witnessing the Fall of the American Empire?", The New Republic, March 7, 2018.
- Heisbourg, F., Ischinger. W., Robertson, G., Schake, K., Valasek, T., *All Alone? What US Retrenchment Means for Europe and NATO*, Centre for European Reform, 2012.
- Hind, J.G.F., "Whatever Happened to the 'Agri Decumates'?", *Britannia*, Society for the Promotion of Roman Studies, Vol. 15 (1984).
- Historia Augusta, *Alexander Severus*.
- Historia Augusta, *Aurelian*.
- Historia Augusta, *Caracalla*.
- Historia Augusta, *The Lives of Carus, Carinus and Numerian*.
- Historia Augusta, *The Two Gallieni*.
- Historia Augusta, *The Two Maximini*.
- Historia Augusta, *Lucius Verus*.
- Historia Augusta, *Marcus Aurelius*.
- Historia Augusta, *Probus*.
- Hodgson, N.,"The British Expedition of Septimius Severus", *Britannia*, Society for the Promotion of Roman Studies, Vol. 45 (2014).
- Holder, P., "Auxiliary Deployment in the Reign of Hadrian", *Bulletin of the Institute of Classical Studies Supplement 81: Documenting the Roman Army*, July 2003.
- Hummer, H.J., "The Fluidity of Barbarian Identity: The Ethnogenesis of Alemanni and Suebi, AD 200-500", *Early Medieval Europe*, 1998, Blackwell Publishers Ltd, Oxford, 7 (1).
- P. Hurley, "Some Thoughts on the Emperor Aurelian as "Perse-

cutor"", *The Classical World*, Vol. 106, The Johns Hopkins University Press, No. 1 (Fall 2012).

- Isaac, B., "The Meaning of the Terms Limes and Limitanei", *The Journal of Roman Studies*, Vol. 78 (1988).
- Jackson, R.B., *At Empire's Edge. Exploring Rome's Egyptian Frontier.* 2002.
- Jaffe, G., "National Security Adviser McMaster Defends Trump's Approach with Allies as *Tough Love*", *Washington Post*, June 28, 2017.
- Jones, A.H.M., "Capitatio and Iugatio", *The Journal of Roman Studies*, Society for the Promotion of Roman Studies, Vol. 47, No. 1/2 (1957).
- Kahn, H., *Thinking About the Unthinkable in the 1980s*, 1985.
- Kennedy, P., *The Rise and Fall of Great Powers*, Unwin Hyman Limited, London, 1988.
- Kennedy, P., *Grand Strategies in War and Peace*, 1991.
- Kent, R., *The Edict of Diocletian Fixing Maximum Prices*, The University of Pennsylvania Law Review, 1920.
- Kirwan, L.P., "Rome beyond The Southern Egyptian Frontier", *The Geographical Journal*, Vol. 123, No. 1 (Mar., 1957).
- Kroeze, K., Vitoria, A., Geltner, G., *Anti-corruption in History: From Antiquity to the Modern Era*, Oxford, 2017.
- Kuijck, J. Van, *The Integration of Mauretania Tingitana in the Diocese of Hispaniae*.
- Lactantius, *De mortibus persecutorum*.
- Le Bohec, Y., *L'esercito romano di Augusto alla fine del III secolo*, Rome, 2008.
- "Legion I Maximiana", *livius.org*, (retrieved February 16, 2018).
- Lendman, S., Asongu, J.J., *The Iraq Quagmire: The Price of Imperial Arrogance*, Greenview Pub Co, 2007.
- Levy, J.S., "Declining Power and the Preventive Motivation for War", World Politics, Cambridge University Press, Cambridge (UK), Vol. 40, No. 1 (Oct., 1987).
- "Limes Tripolitanus", *livius.org*, (retrieved February 17, 2018).

- Littman, R.J., Littman, M.L., "Galen and the Antonine Plague", *The American Journal of Philology*, The Johns Hopkins University Press, Vol. 94, No. 3 (Autumn, 1973).
- Livadiotti, U., *Herodian (7, 2, 1-8), le megístai eikones di Massimino e la guerra germanica del 235*, Thiasos, 4, 2015.
- Lobel, J., "Preventive War and Lessons of History", *Less Safe Less Free: The Failure of Preemption in the War on Terror*, University of Pittsburgh Law Review.
- Luttwak, E., *The Grand Strategy of the Roman Empire* (1976), Bur Rizzoli, 2017.
- Luttwak, E., *The Grand Strategy of the Roman Empire* (1976), Bur Rizzoli, 2016.
- MacDonald, P., Parent, J.M., "Graceful Decline? The Surprising Success of Great Power Retrenchment", *International Security*, Vol. 35, No. 4 (Spring 2011).
- MacDowell, S., *Late Roman Infantryman 236-565 AD*, Reed Consumer Books, London, 1994.
- MacKendrick, P.L., *The Dacian Stones Speak*, The University of North Carolina Press, 2000.
- Martin, J.P., "Sol Invictus: Des Sévères à la Tétrarchie d'après les monnaies", *Cahiers du Centre Gustave Glotz*, Editions de Boccard, Vol. 11 (2000).
- Mathew, G., "The Character of the Gallienic Renaissance", *The Journal of Roman Studies*, Vol. 33, Parts 1 and 2 (1943).
- Maurizio, *Strategikon*.
- Mazzarino, S., *La fine del mondo antico* (1959), Bollati Boringhieri, 2016.
- "Mobene (Qasr Bshir)", *livius.org*, (retrieved February 17, 2018).
- Mokyr, J., "Review: On the (Alleged) Failures of Victorian Britain", *The Journal of British Studies*, Vol. 28, n°1 (Jan. 1989).
- Münkler, H., *Imperi. World Domination from Ancient Rome to the United States*, il Mulino, 2012.
- "Narseh", *iranicaonline.org*, (retrieved November 22, 2018).
- "National Security Adviser McMaster Defends Trump's Ap-

proach with Allies as *Tough Love*", *Washington Post*, June 28, 2017.

- Neusner, J., Chilton, B., *Religious Tolerance in World Religions*, Templeton Press, 2008.
- Nischer, E.C., "The Army Reforms of Diocletian and Constantine and Their Modifications up to the Time of the Notitia Dignitatum", *The Journal of Roman Studies*, Society for the Promotion of Roman Studies, Vol. 13 (1923).
- Nordgren, I., *The Well Spring of the Goths: About the Gothic Peoples in the Nordic Countries and on the Continent*, iUniverse, Inc. New York Lincoln Shanghai, 2004.
- Oates, D., "The Roman Frontier in Northern 'Iraq", *The Geographical Journal*, Vol. 122, No. 2 (Jun., 1956).
- Oborn, G. T., "Why Decius and Valerian Proscribe Christianity?", *Church History*, Vol. 2, No. 2 (Jun., 1933), Cambridge University Press, Cambridge (UK).
- Oltean, I.A., *Dacia: Landscape, Colonization and Romanization*, Routledge, 2007.
- Oost, S. I., "The Alexandrian Seditions under Philip and Gallienus", *Classical Philology*, The University of Chicago Press, Vol. 56, No. 1 (Jan., 1961).
- Parker, G., *El ejército de Flandes y el Camino Español 1567–1659*.
- Pennington, M., "Pentagon Says War in Afghanistan Costs Taxpayers $45 Billion Per Year", *PBS*, February 6, 2018.
- Pliny the Elder, *Natural History*.
- Polfer, M. "Postumus (A.D. 260-269)", *roman-emperors.org*, (retrieved February 14, 2018).
- Procopius, *History of the Wars*.
- Prodromídis, P.I., *Another View on an Old Inflation: Environment and Policies in the Roman Empire up to Diocletian's Price Edict*, Centre of Planning and Economic Research, Athens, February 2006.
- Rance, P., "The *Fulcum*, the Late Roman and Byzantine Testudo: the Germanization of Roman Infantry Tactics?", *Greek, Roman, and Byzantine Studies*, 44 (2004).
- Rasler, K., Thompson, W.R., "Relative Decline and the Over-

consumption-Underinvestment Hypothesis", *International Studies Quarterly*, Wiley, Vol. 35, No. 3 (Sep., 1991).

- Rinaldi Tufi, S., *Archeologia delle Province Romane*, Roma, 2007.
- Rocco, M., *Persistenze e cesure nell'esercito romano dai Severi a Teodosio I: ricerche in ambito socio-politico, istituzionale, strategico*, University of Padua, 2011.
- "Roman Limes: Frontier Line of the Roman Empire in the Iron Gate Area", *danube-cooperation.org*, (retrieved February 17, 2018).
- (Rufus) Festus, *Breviarium rerum gestarum populi Romani*.
- Ruffolo, G., *Quando l'Italia era una superpotenza*, Einaudi, 2004.
- Sabbatani, S., Fiorino, S., "La peste antonina e il declino dell'Impero Romano. Ruolo della guerra partica e della guerra marcomannica tra il 164 e il 182 d.C. nella diffusione del contagio", *Le Infezioni in Medicina*, 2009, Bologna, n. 4.
- Savio, A., *Monete Romane*, Jouvence, 2002.
- Scheid, J., *La religione a Roma*, Laterza, Bari, 1983.
- Scheidel, W., Friesen, S.J., "The Size of the Economy and the Distribution of Income in the Roman Empire", *The Journal of Roman Studies*, Society for the Promotion of Roman Studies, Vol. 99 (2009).
- Schilling, R., *Rites, Cultes, Dieux de Rome*, Klincksieck, Paris, 1979.
- Senofonte, *Hellenica*.
- Sigman, M.C., "The Romans and the Indigenous Tribes of Mauritania Tingitana", *Historia: Zeitschrift für Alte Geschichte*, Franz Steiner Verlag, Bd. 26, H. 4 (4th Qtr., 1977).
- Sirago, V.A., "Diocleziano", *Nuove questioni di storia antica*, Milan, 1967.
- Smith, R.E., "The Army Reforms of Septimius Severus", *Historia: Zeitschrift für Alte Geschichte*, Franz Steiner Verlag, Bd. 21, H. 3 (3rd Qtr., 1972).
- Sordi, M., *I cristiani e l'impero romano*, Jaca Book, Milan, 2004.
- Southern, P., *The Roman Empire from Severus to Constantine* (2001), Routledge, London, 2015.

- Stankovic, E., *Diocletian's Military Reforms*, Acta Univ. Sapientiae, Legal Studies, 1,1 (2012).
- Tacitus, *Agricola*.
- Tacitus, *The Annals*.
- Tacitus, *The Histories*.
- Temin, P., *The Roman Market Economy*, Princeton University Press, 2013.
- Thompson, E.A., "Constantine, Constantius II, and the Lower Danube Frontier", *Hermes*, 84. Bd., Franz Steiner Verlag, H. 3 (1956).
- Thompson, W. R., Zuk, G., "World Power and the Strategic Trap of Territorial Commitments", *International Studies Quarterly*, Wiley on behalf of The International Studies Association, Vol. 30, No. 3 (Sep., 1986).
- Thucydides, *The Peloponnesian War*.
- Tudor, D., "La fortificazione delle città romane della Dacia nel sec. III dell'e.n.", *Historia: Zeitschrift für Alte Geschichte*, Franz Steiner Verlag, Bd. 14, H. 3 (Jul., 1965).
- US National Security Strategy 2015.
- US National Security Strategy 2017.
- Varro, *De lingua Latina*.
- Vegetius, *Epitoma Rei Militaris*.
- Wacher, J.S., *The Roman World*, Taylor and Francis, Vol.1, 2002.
- Wassink, A., "Inflation and Financial Policy under the Roman Empire to the Price Edict of 301 A.D.", *Historia: Zeitschrift für Alte Geschichte*, Franz Steiner Verlag, Bd. 40, H. 4 (1991).
- Watson, A., *Aurelian and the Third Century* (1999), Routledge, London, 2003.
- Wheeler, E.L., *Methodological Limits and the Mirage of Roman Strategy: Part I*.
- "Why Afghanistan is More Dangerous Than Ever", BBC News, September 14, 2018.
- "Why US Marines are deployed to Australia's far north – Darwinian Evolution", *The Economist*, February 6, 2018.

- Wozniak, M., "The Obama Doctrine - U.S. Strategic Retrenchment and its Consequences", *Securitologia*, No 2/2015.
- Zonaras, *Extracts of History*.
- Zosimus, *New History*.
- Zumbrunnen, J., *Silence and Democracy: Athenian Politics in Thucydides' History*, 2010.

Table of Contents

Made in the USA
Columbia, SC
29 November 2020